My Name is Also Freedom
Young Readers' Edition

How One Woman's Flight to Freedom
Made International Headlines

Shari Ho with Melodie Fox

Square Tree Disclaimer

The story you are about to read is based upon the true-life events of Ho Hsiao-feng, also known as Shari Ho. Shari tells her story as she remembers it: her childhood as a young, native Paiwan child of Taiwan, being sold into slavery, her abuse at the hands of her captors, both in Taiwan and the United States, and of her escape and new life in the United States.

All names have been changed to protect the privacy of those involved. Shari did not write this story to place blame or to single out those who played a part in her enslavement or mistreatment, nor do she or others intend to profit from these events. Rather, Shari aims to shine a light on the plight of human trafficking survivors and the crime of human trafficking that still exists today. This story is meant to promote awareness and to encourage those who suspect a person is involved in the crime of human trafficking to speak out about such suspected activity. Furthermore, Shari hopes her story will teach forgiveness, aid in the healing of human trafficking survivors, and bring healing to all.

If you suspect a person is a possible victim of
human trafficking, please call:
National Human Trafficking Hotline
888-373-7888

To all of the Survivors who have not yet found a voice to tell their story, to those fighting selflessly to end human trafficking, and to those brave enough to read this story and vow to never be silent again

Table of Contents

Prologue

My name is Shari. This is not the name I was born with and not the name I was called most of my life. I chose this name. It was one of the first things I was able to choose for myself when I found freedom. You see, I am a survivor of human trafficking.

I watch young people today at the mall or walking about and think, "Where are they going with their friends? To school, the movies, or shopping?" I see them laugh with one another and wonder, "What do they hope to do with their lives? Will summer bring a vacation with their family? Will reading a new, exciting book stir a passion in them to change the world?" At one time I longed for school days, for family time, for at least one moment to voice how I felt or to find a passion in life. I was not allowed to do this. I wasn't allowed to go to school, have friends, or speak my mind. I was only to serve or be beaten for not obeying.

I do feel that I am lucky because I am strong and stubborn. I think if I were not, I wouldn't be here today. It is hard to speak about what has happened in my life. It is so very hard. At times, I don't want to think about the past, yet in speaking about it I am made stronger. I feel deep inside that my story can help others. The past is the past, but I am concerned for others that one day may be in my shoes. How can I keep this from happening? How can I help those it has happened to?

All of my family lives in Taiwan, where we grew up very, very poor. People would look at us and think, "They are poor, uneducated, and dirty; they sell their children." It is hard to deny that this was true—and it was this poverty that forced my parents to sell me—but it was so unfair to be treated badly simply because my family was native Taiwanese, from the original aboriginal tribes that once proudly lived and flourished in the mountainous regions of Taiwan. I am now proud of being Paiwan. It is an honorable tribe, rich in culture. But then, and at times today, we were not always treated fairly.

I want to do something to redeem all of this, to make my ancestors proud. Though my language skills are limited, I am determined to tell my story, no matter the obstacles.

When I escaped from that life, I had been a slave doing forced labor for over 20 years. Can you imagine a whole lifetime of being a prisoner? Day after day of being invisible, treated worse than a dog if I made one mistake? I could have stayed in a shelter after I escaped, but I couldn't take another day of feeling like a prisoner, sleeping in a strange bed, eating whatever was given to me. Maybe I would be able to read and write by now if I had. It was my choice. At that time, I didn't want to have to depend on others for my needs anymore. I just wanted to live free.

When my story was the subject of a CNN news report, I became internationally known. Reporters mobbed me everywhere I went. Headlines about my story filled newspapers all over my native Taiwan.

"News that a Taiwanese woman who was forced into domestic servitude in the U.S. ... made headlines around the nation, and has led, as expected, to wide coverage in local media."—China Post, November 29, 2011

"[This] story of abuse sparked a media storm in Taiwan ... 'This kind of humanitarian travesty would not happen nowadays. I can assure you, people in Taiwan are now much more human rights–conscious ... today's Taiwan is different,' said Taiwan's Foreign Minister, Timothy Yang. CNN's Martin Savidge commented, 'For the president of Taiwan himself wants to make the reunion happen ... the story has become a sensation in Taiwan.'"—CNN, November, 2011

"While the melodrama continues to unfold on prime time TV, is [this woman] really Hsiao-feng? Why does she not call her family back in

Taitung? Is she angry with them? Are there any more twists in the story? No one seems to care about the fundamental question, which is why all this happened in the first place." —*The China Post*, Nov. 29, 2011

"Ho Hsiao-feng, the subject of a CNN report on slavery in November, is confirmed to be a Paiwan aborigine from Taitung in Eastern Taiwan, [and has] arrived in Taiwan in the company of her friends, lawyer, and U.S. social workers." —*Taiwan Today*, January 19, 2012

"... A Taiwanese woman who was identified in a CNN Freedom Project report on human slavery last November, left ... Tuesday to return to Taiwan for a family reunion ..." —*Focus Taiwan*, January, 2012

I had no idea what would come from all of this, but I hoped to find the family I had been separated from all of these years. And what if I was able to reunite with them? How would I be able to forgive what they had done and reconnect with them to truly be a family once again?

This is my story. It is a journey that is still not complete but continues moving forward with each day. I am so thankful to those who have helped me in so many ways, and so very thankful to God for how He has turned all of this around. I have been through so much, but at each turn I can see how God was with me, leading me and helping me to be who I am and where I find myself today. I have looked forward to the day I would share this story with you. It has been my passion for so long to write this book and to be a voice for others, those who are survivors of what I have been through and much more. Many people saw what was happening to me but never said a word. It is time to speak out, to no longer be silent! This is not right, to sell another human being, to mistreat a Child of God, to watch and do nothing. This is MY voice speaking on behalf of them all. I need you to speak out with me so our voices can be strong. God is with us. He is always with us.

My Name is Shari, but my name is also FREEDOM.

If you suspect a person is a possible victim of
human trafficking please call:
National Human Trafficking Hotline
888-373-7888

Part I
My Family, My Tribe

Chapter 1

Memories of Home

Tucked between the green mountains of Taitung on the south-east coast of Taiwan and the beautiful blue waters of the Pacific Ocean lies the small quiet village of Dawu Township. Its warm, wind-swept countryside curves along the highway that winds its way up and down the coast. Looking down from the grassy cliffs above to the ocean, small white-capped waves gently slap the shore below. Miles of endless sea spread out, a reminder of just how small we truly are in the vastness of life and how alone we can sometimes feel. Cold and indifferent to our struggles, yet oddly comforting, it flows on. This is the home of my people, the Paiwan. According to myth, this spot is where heaven is said to exist, and the Paiwan tribe (the name also means, 'human beings') have chosen to live for centuries. Although my memory of living here as a small child is hazy, I remember the mountain hikes, the smell of the cool ocean breeze, and my mother cooking rice. I would find myself often dreaming of this "heaven," a world lost to me. My own nation's history, lost to me as well.

Most of my tribe still lives here, along with other indigenous peoples of Taiwan. Some things have changed little over time. You will still see families choosing to cook and eat outside rather than in the small, cramped, hot, and humid homes they live in. They sit and cook and eat and talk about life. However, the clash of modern technology and communal living seems rather odd as family members crowd around several small BBQs, cooking traditional meals, chewing the lip-staining betel nut, all the while talking, texting, and checking out the latest posts on social media on their smartphones. Dogs roam the narrow streets that lie just yards from the wide, main highway. Protected from most of the population and pollution of the big cities by the mountains and the sea, the days are mostly still and quiet, perfectly bridging the past and the present.

Still dotting the mountainside are homes built with whatever supplies that may have been on hand at the time—corrugated scrap metal roofs, large rocks, tarps fastened by rope, which hold walls together, offering weak protection from the rain, along with odd items here and there—nothing that looked like building materials. These homes are much like the home I lived in with my family. But those are slowly disappearing as government funded homes replace them. Living, however, is still pretty simple: a shared bathroom and bedroom, small room to watch TV and large kitchen space that resembles more of a garage, having just the bare necessities such as a stove and sink. It is just enough, but no more.

16

Memories of Home

Beds are still the long, flat platforms, rising less than a foot off the ground, with an enormous mattress flung on top, a little harder than the American in me would like to sleep on. I can remember sleeping with my sisters, sharing the few pillows we had between us, staring at the walls, hoping the scorpions and snakes would not wriggle through to visit while I slept.

Taiwan

Life in Taiwan is not as hard as it was in the early 1980s, at the time that I was born. Then, the poverty in my tribe was unbearable, especially for my father, who had just us girls, no sons. There is so much for me to still learn about—the history, the struggle of my people. I was not allowed to learn about my culture, any culture, when I was a slave. Returning to Taiwan in 2012, I began to learn about my country, about my tribe.

Our history is mixed with such poverty and heartache. In the faded memories I still see inside of me are the shadows of shame—being looked down upon—because we were so poor. Looked down upon for being "from the mountain." They saw only slavery. And why not? We were slaves to the very poor life we led and to how others viewed our poverty. It was not always like this. The Paiwan were a brave and fierce people, whose tattooed hands and warrior skills put fear into all who dared intrude upon their shores.

Taiwan (Formosa as it was known so long ago) was a beautiful gem desired by many nations. China would eventually lay claim to it, but it was the independent spirit of my tribe and other tribes that would provoke an invasion by the Japanese in 1874, leading ultimately to Japanese domination in 1895. Aboriginal tribes such as my own Paiwan resisted the heavy-handed Japanese rule, provoking many deaths.

The Japanese colonization of the island was harsh. It began with a strict period of rule which eventually gave way, just after World War I, to a time where all peoples and races here were treated more "equally" (proclaimed by Taiwanese Nationalists). And finally, during World War II, there was a period of Kōminka, a policy which aimed to turn the Taiwanese into loyal subjects of the Japanese emperor.

After World War I, Japan had begun to grow at such a rate it became desperately in need of resources for its people. Taiwan, with its fertile soil and abundant resources, met this need. The Japanese wanted to compete with the British Empire, hoping to make Taiwan its "model of perfection" of all that they could do. As the Japanese rapidly developed Taiwan, railroads were built, banks were established, ports were completed for shipping, and electric power reached the island. By 1905, Taiwan was considered the second-most developed region of East Asia and was financially self-sufficient, no longer in need of subsidies from Japan's central government.

Under the Pan-Asian beliefs of Governor Shimpei Goto, exports and food production increased by four times, and by 1925,

Taiwan was a major food supplier for Japan's industrial economy. Japan established the health care system, and infectious diseases nearly disappeared completely. As harsh as this rule could be, prosperity accompanied it.

It was during this time that a move to educate (more likely, indoctrinate) the Taiwanese, including all native tribes like my own, began. Mandatory education proved valuable to all Taiwanese, creating the importance of the written word even to today. World War II would see the Chinese regain Taiwan, and by 1952 the transition would be complete.

My Father

It was this push by the Japanese to educate all of Taiwan that gave my father his education, enabling him to read and write. He was the only one in our family, to my knowledge, who had been to school. But although this seemed to be a huge advantage to most, it would have no effect on me. My father was a complicated and often cruel man. I could not understand why he treated my mother so poorly, and as just a very young child, I felt a distaste for him, even in his kinder moments. He was an alcoholic and abusive. Maybe it was the fact that no matter how hard he tried, he could not gain the respect of those in our village, or that he could bring in no steady income for our family, or that he produced no sons. Whatever may have shaped the way he was, it was set in stone by the time I was born, the second of six girls. My father was never able to keep a job, and my mother provided most of the money to keep our family from starving. She worked as hard as she could, but she would never end up making enough to keep my sisters, including myself, from being sold off. She barely generated enough money for those who remained behind to exist on. I was stubbornly defensive towards my father when I saw him drink. He would often fly into a rage, which was aimed mostly towards my mother. I felt strongly protective of my mother. I never felt love for or from my father. He seemed distant and mean, and only later in life would I find out some of his dark past and the reasons he had turned to alcohol to numb his troubled life. Few fond memories have been buried deep, where I can now see his attempt to give us a better life, but then, of course, I could not see it that way.

The TV

I remember once my dad had decided to get a TV for us. We had no money for this, but he brought it home one day, and we were all thrilled! Why on earth had he thought of such an idea when probably meat or some food would've been more practical, I'll never know, but we were excited just the same.

I remember hearing the excitement as they hauled this grey-brown box into the house. I had been outside doing some chore or another when the loud shouts reached me. I ran up the path towards the house, my bare feet stirring up the loose dirt and carrying the small dust cloud I made upward to cling to my already filthy legs. I tore around the corner and stopped short, just in time to see my father and another man haul the TV through the doorway. I really had no idea what all this was about, but I was excited just the same. I pushed past everyone, squeezing between a few legs to get a front-row seat in front of this new thing. The box was a dark, shiny brown with a grayish glass front, curved at the edges. We all crowded around the set, eager to see what most families took for granted.

I heard my father curse a few times as he looked for a place to plug it in. There were some buttons and dials on the right side of the glass screen and after managing to push past us girls, for we were all now crowded in front of the box, he pulled the on switch. It took a moment or two before a faint, blue-gray light formed from the edges and slowly filled the screen. My mother had joined us by now from the kitchen area, curious enough to see this thing and a bit suspicious of how her husband was able to buy such an expensive item. The light glowing from the screen gave way to pictures jumping and changing with great streaks of color. And the sounds! Music and talking and laughter! We watched it all day and into the night, fitting in chores that had to be done in turn, so we wouldn't get into trouble. We all groaned when the fun was over, and it was time to go to bed.

Early the next morning, we heard a banging on our door. It was a man asking for my father. We heard arguing outside and then the man barged in, unplugged the heavy TV set with an angry jerk, and loaded it up onto his small pick-up truck. He was yelling at my father, scolding him, saying, "How did you intend to pay for the thing when you have no money?" He slammed the door of the truck, still mumbling complaints, and took our lovely TV away.

My Name is Also Freedom

My father had a hard life. I never really knew what had made it so hard, just stories about his past, some unfair things he had gone through. I never remember him having a job or going to work at all. He spent most of his time drinking. If he didn't drink, he would shake. He would often look for work, but no one wanted to hire him. I didn't know why he seemed so hated by the people in our village. He had worked at a furniture factory when he met my mother, and it seems something happened that got him into debt. The story went that he had co-signed on a loan for a friend, and his friend did not pay, which made him responsible for the debt. I don't know if the story is true, but it might explain why he struggled with money.

Seeds of Bitterness

My father had also found himself on the wrong end of a lawsuit, which made him bitter. It was after this that his bouts of drinking grew so much worse, and his abuse towards my mother increased. My mother later told me she believed that this was the beginning of selling us children as slaves for money.

Things seemed to get worse for my father as time went by. Survival was tough in those days. I think he blamed my mother for many of the problems we had. All I do know is his drinking would not solve things and would only lead to many more problems. Once, I overheard an argument when mother was taking the washing off the clothesline. Why they were fighting I never did know, but a loud noise drew my attention towards the mountain. The wind was blowing the clothes that still hung on the line. They were flapping harshly in the wind. As they argued, my mother still pulled the clothes off the line, folded the dry ones in half, and put them in the basket. She did not look my father in the eye. Suddenly, I saw my father kick my mother, and I watched as she tumbled down the grassy hillside. I screamed as I ran to where she lay. Relieved to see just a few scratches, I looked back at this man with anger in my eyes. *Why do you treat her this way?!* I fumed inside. My mother was pregnant with my little sister at the time.

I would discover much later that his out-of-control anger and drinking would play a big part in his death.

Hsiao-feng

I was named Hsiao-feng. There is a mythical royal bird in Chinese with a similar name. This magnificent bird is so gentle and giving, it will not take from anyone. Its only food is the dew of the morning mist. It appears only in places that are blessed with peace, prosperity, and happiness, and it hides away in times of trouble. Maybe my parents gave me this name in an effort to bring hope to our harsh family life. Many mornings as I awoke, I rushed to the door to see if the brightly colored bird had made his appearance, but I found only the dew on the ground and the mountain mist hanging low along the path. The disappointment would not keep me from hoping to see it. I would remind myself to keep hoping and be positive. I try to always carry thankfulness inside of me. When I faced terrible times, I thought about what I was thankful for. I am thankful for having hope.

A Seed of Faith

It's funny how the struggles and the hardships of life can create a
tenacity to survive that is almost miraculous. I only lived with my
birth family for a short seven years, but I had a determined spirit in
me that would not be crushed or stolen. I was just as determined to
love as I was to hate, but I also had the wisdom to know that a life
of hate could destroy me from the inside. How often I let the two
battle within me, but peace of mind and love would always win—it
seemed God made sure of that. He spoke to me deep inside my
heart. No one told me He would do this, or that He even existed,
but His spirit was my guide, always keeping me on the right path in
the darkest places of my life. Maybe it was my mother who planted
that seed in me. She was the only one in our family who went to
church. She believed in God, and I was drawn to her faith.

Catholic Church

My mother went to Catholic Church at that time. Maybe it was
these church visits that planted a seed of God in me. In those days, I
went with her. I loved going anywhere with my mother. We walked
mostly or sometimes took the bus. It was just the two of us. How I
wish I could remember the message or what we did in that church!
I remember watching her, seeing her face, wondering what she was
thinking. Voices echoed off the walls as the man up in the front
talked. There was something peaceful about this place. It was always
over too soon, and we would head home.

It's hard to explain, but I knew that God was there somehow.

Chapter 2

Lessons from My Mother

The house where I was born no longer sits atop that grassy mountain cliff in Taitung. The government has done so much to help the tribes and reduce the poverty I knew as a child. More homes, rent-free, are available, and all of them have electricity and more modern comforts than I had then. A few, however, still perch there like my childhood home, built with rocks and tarps and tires. The weather is pretty consistent year-round, mild and more hot than cold, but we do get quite a lot of rain. During the typhoon season, which starts sometime in June and lasts into October, the rain just pours down. I can still remember the nights the rain dripped down on us from the cracks above our heads. We had so many leaks in our ceiling, it was a wonder the roof didn't collapse! Sometimes during this season huge trees would fall to the ground, smashing whatever they fell upon. The water would shove leaves, mud, tree branches, anything in its path, forcefully, like a river, down towards the road, blocking it for any vehicle that tried to pass. Those in the village would work together, even my father, to dig away the debris and thick mud so the road would be clear again.

The rain would also bring out all the insects and creatures that were looking for a place to dry off. That's when the snakes would come into our house. I hated those snakes! They'd wriggle through the small holes they could find in the walls and curl up under the bed. And in the colder winter time, the snakes especially liked the warmth from the fire we made inside.

Once, I was bitten by a poisonous, ten-legged critter. I don't know what sort of bug this was; I just remember I had been sleeping as it crawled up on me. I don't know if I tried to swat it or what, but I felt a sharp pain as the creature bit into me. Of course, going to the doctor was out of the question. My mom simply made a mixture of rice alcohol and smashed ginger root—a messy, wet mix—and put it on my bite. Oh, the pain was incredible! But it wasn't long after that the bite just disappeared. I felt like it was a miracle. God was protecting me. This is how we coped whenever we were sick; we just dealt with it ourselves. We did have people who would donate medicine to our tribe from time to time, but when that wasn't available, we would rely on our own homemade remedies. Amazingly, we all lived and are healthy today.

Our house was pretty primitive and much too tiny for all of us. It had been built with electricity; we just never had the money to pay for it. Others around us used propane gas, but we used fire to cook and for light. We would use the natural sunlight during the day and firelight at night. In winter, it would get so smoky when we'd have a fire inside. My mom would collect the wood, so we'd have it for the winter, stacking it up against a somewhat dry spot near the house. Our house was super small. We had no bathroom in the house. If we had to use the toilet, we went outside somewhere and dug a hole.

I can't remember my oldest sister ever living with us. I saw her only twice, so really, I became the oldest one out of the rest of us five girls. I was helpful to my mom. I swept the floor, which was dirt. Sometimes we had rice. My mom showed me with her hands how much water to put in the big black pot so it wouldn't spill over and it would cook perfectly. I couldn't let the water come to a rolling boil, and I must always keep a careful eye to watch the fire. The first time I cooked the rice, I burnt it. I remember how bad I felt then. "This is what we have to eat," my mom said. I realized how important it was to pay close attention to all she taught me. I made a decision right then that I was never going to burn the rice again!

In the summer, my dad would go hunting for wild pig, deer, rabbit (which I hated the taste of), coyote, and even small wild mice. He would go with most of the men from the village, hoping to get a generous "kill shot." Whoever shot the head of an animal could claim the head, which meant a bigger portion for your family. In winter, we caught fresh fish from the ocean. The biggest problem for us was refrigeration. We had no way to keep the meat fresh, so we had to salt it, hang it up, and dry it. We would enjoy a few meals of cooked fresh meat and then something more like jerky would have to sustain all of us. We all shared. The village rule of sharing meant no matter who killed what, everyone enjoyed the spoils, so it didn't always go too far. My mom used the fat from the animals that we hunted to make the oil to cook our vegetables in. I remember always eating sweet potato tops cooked in that oil. That's how we survived.

"Lunlun"

"Lunlun, Lunlun?" I can still hear my mother call to me. She had often called me this, my tribal name, when she was in a good mood. What it meant, I couldn't tell you. I always thought it had to do with me being so little—I stand barely five feet tall today—but whatever it meant, I knew it meant she loved me. And I loved my mother. She was always so hard-working and generous. She cared for all of us girls and did the best she could in spite of our extreme poverty. "I want you to help me dig up some yams," she'd say. Yams were a regular meal for us. I remember my mother loved to share when her harvest was plentiful.

My Mother

My mother planted a garden each spring so our family would have food to eat. She had such good fortune working in the soil, for the things she planted seemed to love her and grew without much trouble. She would work hard to pull weeds and keep the vegetables from being eaten by bugs and animals. She grew yams, sweet potatoes, and corn. We all ate from that garden. I remember when it was time to harvest. My father, who did not help much at all in the planting or the harvesting, would watch her pull up the root vegetables and the other produce and happily announce to the neighbors that she had plenty to share. He would question her generosity with a warning, "Why do you give to these judgmental people? You see how they treat us! You know that come winter time when you are in need, they will forget what kindness you've done for them and turn a cold shoulder to your lack!" He would finish with a snort and walk away. My mother would give an uncaring look in his direction, shrug her shoulders, and say, "That's okay. I don't care what they do; when I have enough, I'll do it again and share anyway." Nothing would stop my mother from giving when it was in her power to give. If she had it to give, she would, without complaining.

I can still see her feeding one of my younger sisters, who was not well at the time and could not eat for herself. My mother put the food into her own mouth and would chew and chew, making it soft enough, then feed it to my sister so she could regain her strength. Many hardships came our way, but my mother always put us first when she could, and I know she wanted the best for us all.

The Sickness

"Something is not right. Her head is so hot—she is burning up!" my mother told my father. "What am I to do?" he replied. "We have no money for a doctor ... " his voice trailed off. I felt the panic in my mother's words, but I was too little to respond or even to tell her how I felt. I think I was just about three or four years old at that time, and I had suddenly developed a high fever and itchy red spots that slowly covered my baby-soft skin. I was sick, very sick. I knew it, and she knew it, too. I lay there, not moving. My throat was so very sore, and I had a rash that covered my body. "Maah-ma," I cried, but the sounds I made were mostly sobs and groans. The hours of cold, wet rags on my forehead seemed to do absolutely nothing. The year was 1986. My mother didn't know what to do. She had to work to support the family and any extra money, if there was such a thing, was certainly not there for hospital visits.

My mother was working at the National Park at that time as a cook and housekeeper for the workers. She would have to work a week at a time there and often had to take us girls, there were five of us at that time, with her to work. This could be so difficult. My mother often watched the neighbor children when they were in need of a babysitter, but they would never return the favor. "That man is a useless alcoholic," they'd say about my father. "Look at how they live!" However, my mother remained kind and generous and hardworking; she would simply carry my little sister, and the rest of us would walk with her to the mountain to help her work. My mother had gotten us ready to leave for the mountain when she realized that I was too weak to walk myself. "You must help carry your little sister," Mama told one of my sisters. "I must carry Lun-lun. She is too sick to walk." My temperature was up so very high, and nothing would bring it down. But my mother still had to work, or she would lose her job, and we would not eat, so she wrapped me in a blanket and pulled me close to her. I felt so hot, but I let her pick me up and carry me like a bundle of sticks.

Bumping and jostling, I felt the trail under her feet as she carried me down the mountainside towards the road at the bottom.

Lessons From my Mother

There was a woman, she was not of our Paiwan tribe, who owned a small shop at the bottom of the mountain. She had been sitting out front of her shop, drinking some tea, when my mother and my sisters came down from our home. It was this shop woman who brought the seriousness of the situation to my mother's attention. My red, feverish face peaked out from under the blanket I was wrapped in. "What is wrong with your little girl?" the woman asked. She got up from her chair, setting her teacup down and approaching us. She carefully peeled back the bit of blanket that hid one of my cheeks and gasped as she saw my condition. "This girl may have smallpox!" she exclaimed. I was sweating heavily now and was nearly lifeless-looking. She knew my mother was "from the mountain" and couldn't afford the medicine to make me well. She stopped my mother, not letting her walk any further, urging her to take me to the hospital right away. After the woman persisted, my mother took me to the doctor, who gave me medicine to help bring the fever down and to fight the disease. The hospital bill was too much for my mother to pay, so the shop woman paid it. The woman's kindness saved my life that day, and for that I am very thankful. My mother, however, had to work to repay the shop woman.

Paying off the Debt

The shop woman had some property where she raised deer and other animals that needed feeding. So to pay off the debt, my mother would climb to the top of the mountain where the wild grasses grew each day, cut down the tall shoots, and haul the large bundles back down to the woman's property. Many times after I was well, I climbed with my mother. We would cut them the grasses down together, stacking the piles high on our backs, and carefully climb back down to see to it that the animals had their fill. She did this daily for two years. During this time my mother had become pregnant again, so walking up the mountain and cutting the bundles of grass was especially hard work. After she would haul grasses for my debt, she would go to another job in order to provide for our family.

I recovered, but I have always been the smallest in the family. I don't remember the lady who saved my life, nor my hospital stay, but I do remember those early mornings my mother got up before going to work, hauling grass to feed this woman's animals. My mother never complained about doing this.

The Shoes

From time to time, my memories of those early days living on the mountain come back to me. Often, they are often like the patches on a quilt of many different designs and colors, one here and one there, rarely in sequence. But when they come, I try to grasp them firmly, not wanting them to float away. One day, something brought back this memory of me with my mother, going to different places. I can see her face and how the hair fell across her forehead into her eyes. She would hold my hand as we walked towards the bus station. On the way home, we saw the many people who sold things near there. I curiously looked at vendor after vendor, and I spied a pair of sandals for sale. Most of the time I ran around barefoot. These sandals were so pretty, dotted with brightly-colored flowers. "Mama," I bravely asked, "will you buy this pair of sandals for me?" Shoes were such an important thing to own; if you had shoes, you were not so truly poor.

Shoppers were buying all kinds of things on the street, and I could hear their voices asking, "How much for this?" or "How much for that?" The little shopper in me came out right then and there. I knew that somehow my family was different. We worked so hard for the little we had, but I didn't truly understand what poor really meant. My mother gave a tug on my hand as she gently pulled me away from the vendor's wares. "If I buy a pair of sandals for you, Little One, then I need to buy a pair for all of your sisters. I have no money for them all." What she said hit me hard at that moment. I guess she was right, I hadn't thought about my sisters. It was only right to buy shoes for them, too. Turning my head back over my shoulder, I took one last look at the sandals. They were so colorful and pretty. "I am thankful I have all of my sisters rather than having a pair of sandals," I thought aloud. "One day, I will buy a pair of shoes for myself AND for my sisters." I consoled myself with this thought, something I would become very good at when I found myself far from my family and from happiness.

The Apple

Once, on another such trip, my mother and I passed by a display of apples, stacked up in boxes, set up for sale. I looked down at the apples. I wanted to have one so bad! They looked so juicy, and it was a hot day. Ripe apples filled the cart, and the lady selling them reached out a hand to me, holding an apple so I was sure to see it. "Please, Mama, may we buy an apple today?" I begged. My mother waved her hand at the vendor, which I knew meant, 'no.' Looking

33

down at a bin which contained the apples the vendor couldn't sell—those bruised, pecked, slightly rotten on one side—my mother saw the discarded ones. The smell was not as pleasant coming from the bin. Discarded leaves of vegetables, torn packing supplies, milky puddles from tofu vendors, and other garbage lay strewn about nearby. I glanced down as well. "We cannot afford to buy one of those apples, Lunlun," she said, nodding her head towards the lady, "but reach down there in that bin. There is more than half of the flesh left on that apple in there. You may eat that." I looked at the apple in the garbage. I was hungry, so very hungry. I just kept looking into that garbage bin. I couldn't do it. The apples were spoiled, and I just couldn't bring myself to reach down towards them. Suddenly, several dogs burst from out of nowhere, snapping at each other and starting to fight. They knocked several boxes aside as they growled and tore into each other. My mother yelled at the dogs and jerked me away. The rotten apples rolled out onto the dirty street.

My Brother

I remember caring much for my sisters. My oldest sister was not at home so, as the second-oldest of our family, I was expected to look after my sisters. My mother did have sons from her first marriage, and I do remember my older brother coming to visit. All of her sons were much older and did not live with us. It was usually me and all of my younger sisters at home.

My older brother was very nice. He did visit every so often, and when he did, he always brought food—lots of food! I thought, "He is such a kind brother to bring all this food to us!" He would bring fruit and vegetables and even sometimes meat. I looked forward to his visits and remember thinking to myself, "I want to be this kind of a big sister to my family, one who brings gifts and helps them when they are in need."

My Sisters

My mother and father were constantly looking for work, which meant they would be gone for hours, possibly long after the sun had gone down. Though I was only five or six years old, I was in charge while they were gone.

My mother had taught me many things: to clean the house, wash the clothes, scrub the dishes, sweep the floor, and of course to cook and make rice. She also taught me how to make a fire. We didn't have a working stove at the time, so we had a place outside where we set up some rocks. My mother told me, "You find three rocks. Make them into a triangle shape, so the pot can sit on it." I would set the wood just so and get it started. "If we come home too late, you must set the fire up and cook some food for your sisters." If she was really late, I was instructed to lock up the house and stay inside with my sisters. I know my mother trusted me to do this. I was so little, but she knew I could do this.

I can remember one time when my parents were out looking for work, and I was getting things ready to cook dinner. We had gone out and picked some vegetables from the garden. We rinsed the dirt off, and I got the knife to cut them up for the pot. All of my sisters were sitting so close to me as I started chopping. "Chop,

35

chop, chop ... Oh, no!" I cried, as I cut into my 5th sister's hand with the sharp knife. I did not see a lot of blood, but the cut was very bad. I remember that she really did not cry much. Just then, my mother and father came home. They saw what had happened, grabbed my sister up, and took her quickly down to the doctor. She had to get stitches for that cut, and she still has the scar on her hand to this day. My mother was not angry with me. She said, "You did your best." You know, there were so many times after I was sold as a slave that I felt hate towards my mom, but when I remember this I think, "My mom is not that bad. She really did teach me so many things in the short time I was with her."

The Mountain Lily

Living near the mountains would bring many tourists to the area and provide different jobs for my mother. She cleaned rooms and did other work to meet our family's needs. I remember once when she traveled to the mountain she returned with a lily in her hand. Fields of them grew at one time, high up on the mountain top. This flower is so big and beautiful, a deep orangey-red and yellow, like the colors of the rising and setting sun—fiery, comforting, brilliant. She said, "Close your eyes and stretch out both of your hands, Lunlun." I obeyed her. As my tiny hands reached out towards her, I felt the moist petals, tender and crisp, and caught the faint, fragrant scent. "Do you know what this means?" my mother asked me. I opened my eyes and looked at my beautiful treasure. It filled my two tiny hands, its long, finger-like petals poured over my own fingers, yet I was careful not to drop it to the ground. "I do not know, Mama," I replied. My mother seemed rather serious about this answer. She stared into my eyes as if to say, 'This is very important, Little One, you must not forget this," and said, "This flower, the Mountain Lily, is both beautiful and strong. It grows high up on this mountain. It takes me a long while to hike up far enough in order to find this lovely flower. I want you to be like this flower—pretty, yet strong. You must be *strong*." Then she continued, "This flower is not easily crushed. It withstands the rains and the harsh wind yet remains perfect, whole, pure, and bright. Even long after I have picked it and made the long journey to carry it down to you, it remains big, beautiful, and strong."

Last Supper

I had just turned seven years old. I wish I could remember what day or what month it was, but I can't. Once I left my family to live as a slave, that day would not be acknowledged in any way, so I never knew how old I was for sure. It was not really the custom to celebrate a birthday or holiday that I could remember in my family, so I didn't understand what was happening when one day after my mother had come from the market, she began busily cooking an unusually large meal. "Is tonight special?" I heard my 4th sister ask. There was no reply, but all of us girls, with the exception of my oldest sister, helped with the cutting of vegetables and the preparing of the food. We did not often eat all together. My mother was breastfeeding my youngest sister, who was still just a baby, and my mother, knowing there was never enough food for us all, was always the last to eat. Meat was not a regular dish for dinner, for it was too expensive or hard to come by. We didn't have enough money to buy and raise chickens, so it was a rare occasion we had meat like chicken. We all loved rice, which was also hard to come by. More often, we ate a type of porridge instead, which I remember my mother made in a large pot. That was our usual dinner. But on this night, we all sat together. The smells were incredible! For the first time, I can remember chicken cooking away and rice—the largest pot of rice I have ever seen—steaming away. The delicious smells pushed the questions of "why" or "what" that had popped into my head earlier far away. All I knew was this was how I wanted things to be always. Maybe things were changing. Maybe the bad times were leaving and new good times of chicken and rice were taking its place. My heart hoped, and I nearly spoke my thoughts aloud. I watched my mom as she took each piece of chicken and carefully wrapped it in a bitter leafy vegetable and placed in on a plate to serve to our family.

"Do you know why we are having this big meal with chicken and rice?" my mother asked. Not expecting anyone to answer her question, she quickly answered it herself. "It is because your older sister is working hard, and this money she has earned has bought this feast for all of us." All my thoughts were on the meal and my family that surrounded the table. My heart was so full of joy as I thought of us being here as a family. There was food for us all, and each could have plenty, as it should be. I did not know this would be the last meal I would ever eat with my family. This was the last time I would laugh and eat and feel full inside. It would be twenty years until I would lay eyes on most of those in this room again.

Lessons From my Mother

As I bit into the chicken it tasted bitter, for the herb surrounding it touched my lips. "Mama, something is wrong here," I said. "The chicken is no good. It is spoiling the meat," I announced, disappointedly. I remember the way my mother looked at me. It was a look I had not seen before. She was serious and seemed just a bit sad. How could she feel anything but happiness? We had such a feast in front of us and everything seemed perfect for once. After a moment, she spoke, but I did not expect the answer she gave. "Life is like this meal, Lunlun. It is sweet and good, but bitter and hard. Your life will be like this, too. Always be patient; endure and overcome because tomorrow will always be better. Beneath the bitter herb is tender meat, to make you strong. Do not stop at the first bite; keep eating. Tomorrow *will* be better. You must remember this meal. You must remember this night. Remember my words when times seem too bitter to bear. Keep yourself strong with this thought."

We all ate, and the meal was good. We would be full, but we ate with less joy after that. Something was different about this night. I think I knew things were never to be the same, although I was not quite sure why. I closed my eyes, taking a picture of the scene in my mind. I was determined to remember it, and what my mother taught me that night.

Chapter 3
Take Me!

I have always had a deep love and longing for my family. The memories I have of living with them in the beautiful green mountains of Taiwan are like small puffs of smoke that appear and are so real, but as I reach out to grasp them, they slip through my fingers. Many times, as I mindlessly went about the chores I had to do every day as a slave, I would think about my family—not just the whys of how they came to give me up—but what had happened to each one of them, to my mother and my sisters.

Although I was so small, I was fierce when it came to standing up for what was right, and I was very protective of my little sisters. I would see my parents fighting and jump right in, defending my mother and talking back to my father. How often he would chase me around, threatening to beat me if he caught me! I could not let a wrong go unnoticed. It would take years to get that fighter in me to come out again after my years of slavery, but it was

41

in there, waiting for an injustice to rise, and me to rise with it.

The conversation is cloudy, but I remember talk of sending my littlest sister away. She was just a baby at that time. They talked of selling her or "adopting" her out, more likely, for money, which was no different from selling her. My parents were arguing, like they did nearly every day. My father could be so violent. He would push and shove my mother, holding nothing back, until she was bruised or would fall to the ground. I heard them talking about my little sister. Were they planning on sending her away? I couldn't bear the thought of never seeing her again. What if she were to go to a home where they were mean to her, or worse? I felt my face hot with anger. If I thought I could, I would fight my father and not let him do this thing. But I was just a child. I knew he could hurt me or take it out on my sisters or mother. I heard someone calling my father from the doorway. I saw a man and woman standing just outside. Were they the ones who were coming to take my little sister away?

I saw her little face, such a precious little smile, as I scooped her up in my arms and quickly ran, trying to find a place to hide us both. Could I find a cupboard or closet to climb into? Maybe behind the door? I frantically darted about, but I knew it was useless, as they easily found me. "Hand her to me," my father commanded, stretching his hands towards me. "She is so little," I said, trying to sound so bold and grown up. "Sell me first. Sell me." My anger turned to tears as I turned and faced my mother, still holding my baby sister tight, begging, pleading between the sobs, "Take me! Please, take me!" I would've rather been sent away than

Take Me!

to see my little sister torn from me. "Please," I begged again and again, "Please don't sell her ... sell ME!" My mom thrust her hands forward and tore my baby sister away from me and gave her to the couple. Although she tried to hide them, I saw the tears in my mother's eyes. I stood there, crying, watching these strangers take my little sister away and my parents doing nothing to stop it.

My father jerked me away from my mother, pushing her aside, mumbling some insult at me and my mother as he spat on the floor. He grabbed me by the arm and forced me outside, yelling at me to be silent. He threw me to the ground. "You'll listen to me, or else." He started to tie me to a post that supported the overhang that shaded the house from the hot sun. There was a stick lying nearby that he snatched up to beat me with. My dad bent over me, hand raised to beat me with that stick while I struggled to get away. That is when I heard my mother warn him, "Ok, you do this, you know, she will need to go to the hospital. Do you have money to pay for this?" I felt my dad's angry grip relax a little as he stopped and stood up. A silent moment passed. Then, tossing the stick aside in frustration, he let go of me and walked away. I sat on the ground in a heap, still devastated that I would not see my little sister again. It wasn't but a day or two later that I would also leave my family forever. This battle I fought all alone, but I did not know that the war had only just begun. I thank God that the couple who adopted my sister treated her as their own daughter and never as a slave. I found this out later when I was reunited with my sister when I returned to Taiwan.

43

A Friend of My Father

There was a man in our village who had lost his job. He struggled, just like we all did, to earn enough money to feed his family. Most of the villagers found jobs doing physical labor, working hard; the majority of these jobs lasted only a week or two. This man in our village found something else, something that paid much more and required much less sweat or strength. This man was a friend of my father.

This man found he could make good money, being a broker of sorts, selling children to work in factories or other places. I remember seeing this man when I returned to Taiwan years later to find my family. He looked at me as if he saw a ghost and ran from me. The whole time I was there, I was told, "That man, the one who sold you, is very afraid of what you might do to him. He will not show you his face again." If the law on his crimes had not run out at that time, his fears would be very real. I was ready for him!

My father was so very desperate for money. He was also a very angry man. He blamed my mom for all the bad luck and troubles he had encountered. Yes, I was his flesh and blood, just like the rest of his daughters, but I guess he blamed us, too, for the way things had turned out. After talking to his friend, he found a way to pay his debts and have enough money to live on—at least for a little while.

"Let's go," my dad commanded me one morning. "Get in the car." A beat-up looking sedan sat parked down below our house,

44

Take Me!

on the side of the road. "Come on, I said, let's go!" he insisted. My mother gave me a nod that I was to hurry and obey my father. I ran down the mountain and skidded to a stop in front of the open back door of the car. I was scared, but I got into the backseat.

My dad and this man drove us to the city and around all that day, from factory to factory. "We can try these places first," he told my dad. We'd stop and go inside, my dad trying to convince the owner about what things I could do. But the reply was always the same, "She is too little."

We tried place after place, and it was always the same response, "She is too little." So, the man finally drove us back to the village. "I'll let you know what I hear. I have to check on a few more places ... " his voice trailed off. He said goodbye to my dad and sped off.

It was maybe a day or two later when my dad's friend came back to our house.

"I found this lady who just came back from the United States. Most of her grown children live there, her son's kids, too. They bought a home there. Her daughter just got divorced and remarried an American. They have money. Lots of money. This lady called me and said she could use a helper for around the house and can pay good money," he explained with a grin, "Sound good?"

Chapter 4

Yesterday, Today

Many in western cultures do not know much about human trafficking. Because of its location, human traffickers see Taiwan as a marketplace for men, women, and children from all over the world —Japan, Australia, Vietnam, Thailand, China, and the Philippines, as well as the United Kingdom and the United States—to be sold and used. They hope to take advantage of the poor or hurting for the purpose of forced labor and sexual exploitation. Human traffickers use tricks such as promising good jobs or fake marriages to entice their victims. The human traffickers work through recruitment agencies and brokers in order to find people to work in hard labor jobs or in prostitution. Many victims are promised money, help for their families, or hope for a better life, only to find themselves unable to break free from their "contract." They become victims of abuse or are forced to repay their traffickers for the "debt" they owe. They are stuck and without hope that they will ever see their families again or even escape their slavery.

This was commonplace many years ago in Taiwan. Today, mostly due to legislation such as Taiwan's Immigration Act and the Victims of Trafficking and Violence Protection Act of 2000 (TVPA)—a federal statute passed into law in 2000 by the U.S. Congress, signed by President Clinton, and later reauthorized by presidents Bush, Obama, and Trump—Taiwan is now a Tier 1 Country, which means Taiwan's government fully complies with the TVPA minimum standards. These include improving efforts to investigate and prosecute trafficking cases, enhancing legal protections for trafficking victims, and approving a budget plan of $12.6 million for victim protection measures. The Taiwanese government has also made a tremendous effort to help indigenous tribes and prevent the extreme poverty that led my family into human trafficking.

Still, Taiwan remains a place many traffickers are drawn to today. As I have said, my family was so very poor, and because my parents, especially my dad, struggled to find work, selling one child to gain enough money to keep the family going was a choice for them and many families who were in the same situation as we were.

As a broker, my father's "friend" got rich off of charging a large fee for selling his own tribal people. The war to end slavery still wages, and I did not realize how involved I was to become in it.

Part II
I Am Sold

Chapter 5

The Contract

I can't really remember the details or much about the circumstances of when I was sold to The Old Lady as her slave. It hadn't occurred to me that all that driving from factory to factory in the days before was to try to sell me to one of them. I remember my father telling me that there was this old woman who needed help to clean and cook and that I was going there to help her for a while. I remember the long drive but had no idea where I was going.

Big City, Big Changes

We arrived in Taipei. Such a big city! We drove down a small street and got out of the car. "Come with me," my father commanded, as we walked towards the door of a tall building. His "friend" knocked on the door. When it opened, we climbed the stairs and entered an apartment. It was there I saw her for the first time.

The Old Lady had white hair that was combed back into a

tight bun. I knew she was old, but her skin looked soft and supple, much younger than a person her age. She was so clean and neat looking, and her clothes were beautiful. The house looked and smelled new, and it was much more modern than any houses in our village. There was a bathroom, many other separate rooms, and lots of furniture. While my father talked, The Old Lady kept a serious face as she listened to him and his broker friend. To me, she was just an old woman in need of a helping hand around the house. I could see the disappointment on her face as she saw my size and how young I was. I never thought of myself as being too little to really do much of anything. I was always doing chores at home, and we all worked hard to do the work we needed to do, no matter how big or small we were. I liked being helpful. I was very good at watching how something was done and then being able to do it perfectly.

But The Old Lady thought I was useless. "She is too little to help me," she complained to my dad. "I'll have to give her a bath and take care of *her*!" "No, no," he insisted. "At home she can do a lot of things. She can do all the chores needed around the house." But The Old Lady still seemed uncertain. "Watch," he pulled me towards him. "She knows how to sweep the floor." My dad looked around as The Old Lady quickly grabbed a broom and gave it to me. I swept the whole room. Back and forth I pushed that broom, which was just as tall as I was, until the floor was swept clean. The Old Lady would later tell me, "I tested you, and you passed the test. That is why I let you come stay with me. But nobody else wants you. If it wasn't for me, nobody would want you."

The Contract

"You must stay here for a while, helping The Old Lady," my father said, as he headed towards the door. "She is like a grandma to you." Then he turned to The Old Lady and his friend. Some final words were spoken, and they left. The door closed. I stood there staring at it and at The Old Lady's back as I heard her lock the door. My heart was pounding. "Well?" The Old Lady said as she turned around to face me. "What else can you do?"

I stood staring at The Old Lady, trying to make sense of what was happening. My parents had sold me to be a slave to this woman, but I had known nothing about any of this. A contract was given to my parents. I had no idea for how long or for how much. My life was drastically changed at that moment, and it would take years for me to fully understand it all. I was put to work right then serving this Old Lady in whatever she wanted me to do. Her words were harsh from this first day on, and she would constantly remind me of who I was: *her slave*.

My New "Family"

Dreary, dark buildings that towered above me filled the narrow street. The Old Lady's son owned one of them. It was several stories high and stood across from several bars and other less than reputable businesses. The Old Lady and I lived on the first floor of this building by ourselves while her son and his girlfriend lived on another. The son rented out other floors to various tenants, and the top floor was mostly storage for The Old Lady's son's business. "You must help 'grandma' with whatever she needs you to do," were my father's last words to me. I pulled the window curtain closed as The

Old Lady had told me to, for it was late, and my chores for her had not yet been completed. I would have to rub her legs and pat her hand late into the night, a routine that would continue until the day I left her. Those in search of a drink or two visited the bars across the street that were squeezed in between the buildings that housed people and the questionable 'nightlife.' It was not a scene that a small girl should see out the window. I counted down the days, hoping each would be my last here, for my mom had assured me when I left with my father, "In ten days I will come and bring you home. You know how to count, Lunlun? Ten days," my mother had promised. "She will come back for me," I whispered to myself as I blocked out the drunken voices calling to one another outside. I closed my eyes. "She promised me she will come back for me."

Get to Work

"Make some rice," The Old Lady barked at me, all the while mumbling loudly under her breath how small and useless I was and how she would have to watch everything I did around her house. My days would begin early, before the sun would rise, and she made sure the work was non-stop. As I prepared the rice, my thoughts went back to the day my mother had taught me how to make rice for the first time. I had been making rice since I was old enough to hold a pot. I carefully filled the pot with water. It was heavy, and I was so very small, but I did it. Too small to reach the stove, I pushed a small stool close to the stove to stand on and continued my task. I was a very fast learner: tell me or show me something just once, and I could do it. Whatever the chore might be, I worked hard to please the grandma, all the while longing for my mother to come and get me and take me back home.

Weeks passed, and it became difficult to hide my sadness from the grandma. "What is wrong with you?" she prodded one day. "I don't want to look at this sad face anymore! It makes you slow in your work." Holding back the tears, I began to complain that weeks had now passed without any sign of my mother returning for me. "My father told me Mama would come for me. She promised," I choked, my throat painfully tight. It was all I could do not to burst out crying. "Your mother is never coming for you!" the grandma fired back, her words nearly slapping me across the face with their impact. "I paid good money for you—not that you were worth what I gave that man; you are so small. Why I paid so much, I don't know! If you want to go back there you must pay me what I paid him!" The Old Lady demanded, "Your parents sold you for $10,000 NTD[1]. From now on, you will stay here. You will never go back home again!"

So that was it. I had been sold. I was only seven years old, but I knew what that meant. My family had truly sold me as a servant, a slave to this bitter and angry old lady, my 'grandma' as I was to call her. My heart sank deep inside me like a stone. At that point, the real person I was—the strong, confident fighter—curled up from this betrayal, and I just zipped her up inside like a jacket. How does a seven-year-old little girl understand all this? I had to have love, acceptance, a family. And although this grandma of mine would never treat me as family, I tried to do all I could to get that love and

---

1   That is about $310.00 U.S. dollars.

acceptance from her. I kept that tenacious, outspoken fighter locked up and silent. I, Little Lunlun, disappeared, and the slave, Hsiao-feng, was born.

Life with "Grandma"

"How many times must I tell you to get up and make my breakfast!" The Old Lady barked, the way she always talked to me. She had a way with every word she said of making me feel stupid, incompetent, and worthless. I carried those words on my shoulders like a beast of burden, nearly hunched over from the weight of them. She kicked the mat I laid on and I jumped to my feet. It was one of the first times I had ever overslept. My routine was to be up before five to make The Old Lady her breakfast, lay out her clothes for the day and begin my chores for the household, which included cleaning the floor we lived on, the second floor that had an office where the son conducted his business, and all of the rooms in this large building. My days were long and every minute not cleaning was spent attending to The Old Lady's needs. I was up before dawn and rarely went to bed before midnight. I was not given a bed at all to sleep in, but a mat was laid on the floor in The Old Lady's bedroom and only on truly cold nights was I given a shabby, old blanket to keep warm. I had no pillow, but found some smelly old rags that I managed to fashion a sort of pillow out of for myself. The smell of them both made me sick. As I jumped to my feet, I clumsily made my way into the kitchen and prepared her first meal. Of course I was never allowed to sit at the table and eat with The Old Lady, nor was I allowed to cook for myself but waited for her to finish, cleaned up her dishes and then took whatever leftovers that were there, and squatted in the corner to eat my 'breakfast.' I was truly a slave in every sense of the word—nothing to call my own and no comforts in life to speak of. The Old Lady would never see me as family, although for the sake of outsiders she called me 'granddaughter.' She barely saw me as human, not an ounce of pity would she spare towards me and not a penny would she spend on me as well. I was not allowed to eat out of a bowl *she* might use, nor use a pair of her chopsticks. I had one bowl and one spoon I would use all of my life with her and sometimes, I was only allowed to eat with my hands. "You are a slave," she would remind me almost daily. "You cannot use the same dishes I use. You cannot eat at the same table as me. You are not, and will never, ever be equal to me!"

Life became so very hard living with my "grandma." She was a cruel and demanding woman who was angry all the time. I was small and tried my best to do everything she wanted. At first, I broke a lot of dishes because I was too little to reach into the cupboards. The Old Lady would slap my face when I broke things. No matter how hard I tried to do right for her, she was not satisfied. She was old, her mind was made up that I was not good enough, and I was not going to change that. She would never be pleased with me.

The Old Lady

Though she lacked in compassion, The Old Lady did not lack in taste—especially for fine clothing. She was a woman of wealth. Her son and her daughter both owned properties, and although her husband had died years ago, he must've left her plenty of money to live on. All of her clothes were handmade for her in China of the finest silks. The colors were brilliant and all the fine details of birds and de-signs were hand stitched with care. Every day I laid out her clothes, making sure they matched perfectly. She had lightweight silks for summer to keep her cool in the humid Taipei days, and thicker, insulated outfits for winter when the weather turned much colder. Reds and yellows, turquoise and greens—I grew quite good at this task, and it wouldn't be long before my accomplishment received a nod (but of course with a smirk) rather than the usual insults. I believe it was this chore that developed my talent (and the taste) for fine fashion. I just knew what would look good together and how to construct her outfits. In the drudgery of every day, for just a moment, I could pretend I was someone else, living somewhere else, far away from my life.

Living in Taipei was so different than living in my village. Even though the house was better—she had electricity and an indoor toilet—I didn't want to live here with her; I still wanted to go home. Life in the big city could've been exciting, if I were ever allowed outside the walls of The Old Lady's home. The Old Lady had everything. I, on the other hand, lived like the poorest street child. I had come to live with The Old Lady with just the clothes on my back, but even a tiny little girl eventually grows, and soon my clothes and shoes did not fit. She did not treat me as a true grandchild. She ignored my needs for clothes and shoes and school. The Old Lady would blame me for the way I looked, knowing it was her responsibility. I learned quickly to wash out my own clothes each night if I wanted them clean and to pay attention to even the smallest details, so I would not be beaten or yelled at for doing something wrong.

Abuse Begins

My days with The Old Lady were so tiring. I remember her telling me what chores I would do and how to bathe her and wrap her legs. She had so many beauty treatments to keep her skin looking smooth and soft—and it was! She looked so young! I swear, I never did see a wrinkle on her face at all. But for such a little girl as me to serve her needs, be with her every second of the day … I couldn't keep up at first. I remember the first time I helped her bathe. I scrubbed her back and helped her in and out of the tub. She wouldn't go to sleep until I massaged her legs. It was so late at night, yet she insisted I massage her feet as she fell asleep. So I did. I rubbed and rubbed them, but before I knew it I, too, had fallen asleep. I always sat on the floor. I was never allowed to sit on a couch or chair or on her bed. Funny, I remember her room had this red carpeting on the floor. I had to reach up as I massaged her feet. Well, when I fell asleep, I somehow peed myself. She must've woken up and saw that I was asleep and then noticed the wet spot all around me. That's when she had a fit!

"You *will* clean your mess up spotlessly or you will have to lick your pee off the rug!" she screamed. "Did you hear what I said?! You will clean this up, NOW, or lick that pee up off my carpet!" She was ranting and raving and acting like a crazy person. I cried and cried and finally said, "I am so sorry, Grandma, so sorry. Don't be mad. I will clean it. I will clean it." I quickly found some rags and began cleaning it. "You are an animal! How come you peed the floor like an animal?!" She continued her tirade, "Clean this up, NOW!" I was so tired, it was after midnight, but I cleaned it. I cried all the while, but I cleaned it up.

My Hair

"Sit still!" she demanded, as she grabbed my ear, pulling my head
and neck to the left as she hacked at my hair with a pair of scissors. I
watched the soft dark clumps fall to the ground. A few stray strands
landed on my thigh, and with the jerk of my head from The Old
Lady's harsh grasp, more hair fell upon my toes. I sat still, angry,
holding back my frustrated tears. The Old Lady forced me to have
my hair cut this way. She didn't want me to look like a girl. She cut
it so short. I didn't want to see what I looked like when she finished.
"Clean this up!" she demanded, as she pushed me from the chair,
apparently done with me. "Sweep up every bit of it, you lazy girl." I
reached my hand behind my neck and felt the bare skin, as I brushed
away the bits of hair that had begun to make me itch. This was how
my hair would always look from now on: short, choppy, boy-like.
This is how I looked in the only pictures taken of me when I was
a child. And pictures were taken. I think now they were done to
prove that I was just a happy granddaughter, not an unhappy slave
girl, separated from her real family. I looked happy in most of those
pictures. The clothes I wore in them were cleaner, better than the
clothes I wore before. They tried to show I was happy; how could I
be a slave? I was smiling, but I had to. I did like to smile—it lights up
my whole face. You can see this whenever I smile. I remember this
one picture The Old Lady sent to my sisters of me in a red sweater.
I saw that picture years later on the news. I felt angry inside when I
saw it, knowing how I felt then. It was all such a lie. As I grew older,
the pictures started to show the despair inside me. In one picture

taken of me when I was about ten years old, my smile is missing. You can see that the light inside me had grown so very dim.

I look back and think, "There was something very wrong with that Old Lady." At times, her behavior towards me was so horrid and bizarre. But through it all I still had love for her, even when I hated her. She was the only family I knew.

No Comfort

Day after horrible day, I'd get up and work. I would clean, cook, and be at The Old Lady's command. I'd think about my mom and dad and what they did. Sometimes I'd cry and miss them so much. Every day was miserable. There were days, though, The Old Lady might show me some kindness, when she saw how sad I was. She would offer maybe five minutes of comfort saying, "Come here, it will be alright. You are ok." She was actually nice to me! Those were good days. I would think, "Oh my God, today is a good day. She is nice to me today. Maybe things will be okay." When I was little, this was easier to take. It was easier to smile, but I wasn't really happy. It wasn't real.

On bad days, I'd be so angry. "I wish they all could be punished!" I'd think. "My mom and dad and this grandma, they deserve to feel how I feel for what they all have done to me!" I'd even be mad at God sometimes. "Why did You let them do this to me? Why do You let this Old Lady treat me the way she does?" I could feel hate just boil inside of me. I would imagine all kinds of terrible punishments to justify how they had treated me, but when I gave in to this bitter anger, my days dragged on in hopelessness. It was a huge weight on my shoulders, pressing down on me—heavier and heavier—until I couldn't bear it anymore. It was as if God was asking me, "Do you feel what the hate is doing to you? Can you carry this day after day and live?" I would carry that hate and then lay it down for a while and feel some relief, but it was always there, baiting me to pick it back up again. I would think of my mother's words, "Tomorrow will be better." I would say that over and over to myself. I was on the edge of tears almost every day. "Okay, I have no mother now, but will this grandma finally care about me?"

School

I remember looking out the window of that apartment, high up over the street, overlooking the older concrete or 'no style' buildings here or there, much like the one I lived in, watching the young people hurrying to school. I wanted to go, too, and often asked The Old Lady, "Why don't I go to school?" Her answer was always the same, that I was too stupid, that school would do no good to someone like me, and so on. My heart would ache as I watched those children, wearing their new school clothes, carrying their backpacks of books and chasing each other as they went down the street.

There was a time when some uniformed men came to the door to check if we were supposed to live in this building. We had to show paperwork proving we were not illegal citizens, as many people would hire undocumented workers. "Why is she not in school?" one of the officers said, pointing to me. I looked at The Old Lady, and she lied, saying, "She is my granddaughter. Her father has not changed the paperwork for her to go to school here yet."

The Contract

Once, when The Old Lady made a trip to visit her daughter, I was to stay in Taipei. We were living in a different building then, I think. The Old Lady had a sister who lived a few doors down and she was to care for me while The Old Lady was gone. This woman had been a school teacher. She was much more understanding than her sister and took some pity on me, bringing some books and teaching supplies to me to give me a few lessons. I remember this little book; it had letters and pictures in it. I had never been to school or watched any TV or movies, so I had not been exposed to any education other than the street signs I had seen out the window or on the way to church or market with The Old Lady. I was grateful for this opportunity, as short as it was, but when The Old Lady returned and discovered what her sister had begun, an argument broke out between them, and her sister never looked after me again. I faintly remember hearing her sister say, "She must have lessons! It isn't right to keep her from school. I can teach her if you don't send her for studies." The Old Lady could be completely unreasonable and dismissive. If she felt that something should not be, then it would not be. The Old Lady always won, so I neither went to school nor received another lesson again after that.

Always Hungry

The Old Lady was so unstable and unpredictable at times. She would get something in her head, mostly a suspicion about what I was up to, and she would punish me. She was obsessed with the idea that I might be stealing her food. I was never allowed to eat anything but her scraps and leftovers, but that was still too good for a 'slave' like me. If I opened the cupboards, she would say, "You cannot just open

63

my cupboards without asking." I'd think, *Why can't I, if I am her granddaughter?* She would get angry and say, "You know why I hate you? Because you do something wrong though I am trying to teach you." I would obey her because I was little and accepted what she said as right. After all, she took me in when my family had chosen to sell me.

Stealing Bread

We always went hiking, and I carried The Old Lady's backpack. One day, on our way back from a hike, we stopped at a store. I was always thinking about food because I was always hungry. I saw some bread, and it looked so good! I looked around to see if The Old Lady was watching and then I stole it. I tried to hide it in the bag I was carrying. I didn't know that the cashier had seen me do this. I was SO hungry. She told The Old Lady, "This little girl stole this bread." The Old Lady apologized to the cashier, but when we got home she began hitting me and pulling my hair.

"How dare you do this after all I have done for you!" she ranted. "You are a thief, and I will teach you not to steal and embarrass me!" She grabbed her cane and began beating me with it until red welts rose up all over my legs. I cried out in pain saying, "No, no, I promise. I won't do it again, please, Grandma, no, no!" She grabbed my hair and pulled me to the ground, yanking my head and twisting my neck, screaming the whole time, "You thief!" I couldn't fight her, for the pain would only be worse. I just lay there like a rag doll. When she had finished her violent outburst, she pushed my head down and walked away. I sat in a heap, crying, my legs throbbing where

The Contract

her bamboo cane had stung me with its sharp, quick blows. I rubbed them as the swollen red marks appeared leaving pinkish red stripes up and down my legs. I cried and cried, wishing I could run someplace and hide, but there was nowhere to go. The tears rolled down my cheek silently, for I knew that if The Old Lady heard me, I might get another beating. I got up and went to the bathroom and found a rag. I knew to put some cold water on each welt so the swelling would go down. I did this quickly because I knew she would come looking for me, and she would not be pleased if I didn't return to my chores.

I could not go to the store with her from that moment on without her embarrassing me, watching me, making a fool of me by saying to everyone who worked there, "I am watching her. This thief won't do anything." She did this every time. I was so humiliated. I never stole again.

Soured Food

I never got enough to eat, so I was very skinny.

The Old Lady was a good cook and although I helped cook, she prepared the main dishes while I watched to learn how. We ate traditional foods like pig leg—for a special occasion or Chinese New Year. She loved to cook chicken. I once opened her refrigerator and saw all of the food The Old Lady had in there. Every shelf and drawer was filled! She was just one person, and her son, of course, but there was so much food! I couldn't help saying, "Wow!" when I saw this. I was tempted, and this is the only time this happened, but I took something and ate it. I don't remember what it was, but I do remember shoving it into my mouth. I was so hungry! I was always so hungry. After she found out—and she always found things out—she started counting everything. If she made some chicken, she counted how many pieces she ate and how many were left. As food cooks, it shrinks down. She would look in the pot and say, "Did you take some? Why is this piece so small? You cut some off and ate it. I see you looking at my food, you jealous thief!"

One day, she began screaming at me this way, "You steal my food! This is how you repay me? I know you took my food!" "Grandma, I did not take your food. I would not do that!" I said, but she didn't believe it, so she slapped me across the face. "My food is too good for you. From now on you will eat only what is spoiled, and NOT my leftovers. They are much too good for you!"

Whatever had soured or had gone bad, she would tell me to eat that. What could I do? I was so hungry I had to eat it. This continued for quite a while, until slowly she changed her mind, and I got more leftovers once again. But she would always put her chewed bones or discarded food on top of the food I ate. I would pull off the half-eaten pieces and pick what I could off for myself. I don't like pork to this day, and I think this is why, because she always left the tough, fatty pieces that she had chewed on for me.

The Lock
When she ate dinner or any meal, The Old Lady—and her son and his girlfriend if they were there—ate at the table. I stood up to eat or

The Contract

sat on the floor. Once, when her daughter was visiting and saw that
I sat on the floor to eat, she asked about it. "Mom, why does she eat
on the floor like that?" The Old Lady answered, "She is dirty, a slave,
she cannot use the same chopsticks as we do. She cannot sit with
us." I would wait until she allowed me to eat. The food would have
a sour smell or bits of mold on the corners, but I had to eat it. I was
hungry. I never ever ate enough to feel full.

I remember once she made sticky rice cakes. She'd always
make ten or six or five or eight of something, never four. Numbers
mean something in our culture. It'd mean bad luck to make four,
especially for the New Year. Bad luck all year! On this day when
she counted, somehow one was missing. "You took that rice cake, I
know you did, you worthless slave!" She became furious! "You want
my sticky rice? You can't control your lust for it?" She grabbed me
around the neck and shoved a ball of the rice into my face, forcing
it into my lips. I choked in her tight grip as bits of the sticky grains
smeared over my face, went up my nose, and lodged between
my gums. "That is the last time you will have my sticky rice!" she
growled. She stomped out of the room. I sat on the floor picking
out the pieces of rice that were stuck everywhere. I wiped the tears
away as I saw her storm back into the room with a lock and a small
chain, which she placed through the handles on the refrigerator.
When she stepped back, she had locked the refrigerator up tight, so
I could not get into it! Can you imagine that! If I needed to cook or
be in the kitchen for any reason, The Old Lady would watch me like
a hawk.

The Toothache

I ate sweets only once a year, at Chinese New Year. There would be a box of candy and I would get one piece. It's funny, I have had only one cavity in my whole life. One day my tooth suddenly started hurting really bad. I had gotten up that morning and felt this dull pain that got worse as the day went on. When I couldn't hide it any longer, I began crying. I cried and cried. I tried to tell The Old Lady what I felt, but of course she would not listen. "Grandma, something is not right with my tooth. There is a lot of pain, and it will not stop." This went on for several months. The Old Lady grew tired at times of my suffering, but her solution was to slap me. "This is your fault! I am nice enough to give you one treat and this is how you repay me?! I am sure you stole more candies when I was not aware of it. You deserve the pain!"

My face grew swollen over time, and it became hard to hide. Six months had passed when The Old Lady's sister noticed something was very wrong. "You must take her to the doctor!" she told her sister. I could see the anger in The Old Lady's eyes when her sister scolded her for waiting so long. She took me to the dentist, be-grudgingly, threatening that I must pay her back every penny. I guess I was very lucky. Although I had to have the tooth removed surgical-ly because it was so badly infected, I was otherwise ok. Eventually, a new tooth grew in its place. When I was very little, I remember some of my teeth were loose and falling out and my dad would pull them out and say, "If you don't, you will not get double." People see me now and look at my teeth and comment how nice they look. "How come you are getting younger, not older?" they say.

Chapter 6

Days, Months, Years

Walking was a daily routine with the Old Lady. She was religious about it. Not a day went by without me trudging beside her, her arm leaning heavily upon my shoulder, her umbrella in hand, more for hitting and poking me with than for keeping her dry from the tropical rains. She was always smartly dressed, whatever the season or activity, with no exception. In winter, she wore her ornately detailed, hand-stitched long coat. In summer, her delicate pastel pants and beautifully embroidered silk jacket flapped in the breeze as we walked on and on. She had this way of carrying herself, a slow, almost parade-like march, as if she were someone of importance. I admired that at times, wishing for her approval, which I never received. We'd get up by 5 a.m. to begin the day. I don't think The Old Lady ever slept in a day in her life. Sometimes I'd daydream of just sleeping until the sun woke up before me, shining its light and warmth over my face, soaking it all in until I'd had enough.

My Name is Also Freedom

I felt tired. I was always tired. Even as a young child, I felt exhausted all the time. I guess I should be grateful for these outings; at least I could get outdoors and be distracted from the grueling household chores I had to do. I was not out on my own, but still, I would be out where there were sights and sounds. Besides, whenever there were people around, The Old Lady was not as cruel to me; she'd never outright hit me in public, other than the constant brutal jabs from her umbrella or cruel pinching of my arms.

This is how we always walked about. To most who saw us passing by, it might have seemed endearing, a grandmother with her grandchild helping her with shopping and such. Whether they knew my plight and turned a blind eye to it, or whether they were completely oblivious to the life I was trapped in, no one said a word. I called her Grandma, so why would they question her?

We had a purpose in where we were going each day and a set way in which to do it. We trekked daily to a natural mineral hot springs spa called Yangmingshan. We would have to walk several blocks, then catch a bus and take the long ride up the hillside towards the springs. I dreaded this. Though The Old Lady was dressed beautifully, I was always in the same clothes, stained from doing chores in them and usually threadbare. I would have to wash all of my clothes by hand and hang them to dry each night, and in the humid Taipei air I couldn't be sure they'd always dry in time. I wore them many times before I washed them, so they smelled. I was very conscious of this as we traveled about—I looked every bit of

Days, Months, Years

the slave I felt like inside.

The Bus

The bus ride was a very long one. Sometimes I had to stand if the bus was quite full. The Old Lady never put me on her lap, nor let me take a seat if she felt someone else deserved to sit other than me. When I sat, I longed to fall asleep, but if The Old Lady saw me with my eyes closed, a sharp poke from her umbrella would bring me back to my unfortunate reality.

I got so hungry on those long rides up the mountain. I rarely ate any breakfast before we went out, maybe a leftover scrap of bread, if I was lucky. Trying my best not to let The Old Lady see me, I would look for leftover food on the bus. The bus would go to the end of its stop before it turned around and headed back up. The driver made everyone get off the bus as it did this. Sometimes people would leave their half-eaten food on a seat, or if I was lucky, a piece of fruit at the bottom of a bag on the ground. One day, someone must've forgotten their lunch. I saw this bag carefully folded at the top just sitting by itself on a seat towards the back. I hurriedly walked towards it, blocking its view from The Old Lady. I put the backpack I carried in front of me and then set it in front of the lunch bag. Unzipping the pack and as quick as I could, I shoved the lunch bag into the back of my bag and closed it. The bus took off. Carefully, when The Old Lady wasn't looking, I stole bits of it, as quietly as I could, as the bus rocked and bumped its way back towards the mountain.

My Name is Also Freedom

When we reached the top, we still had to walk quite a way of a steep hill. Trees lined either side of the road as it twisted upward, which became narrower as it climbed towards the springs. I remember we'd stop at a parklike nature area for a while. Here, many old people sat, sitting upon benches made from large rocks, whose tops had been polished to a shiny flat seat of blues and greens. Similarly made tables resembled more of a real table, round with a pedestal of reddish-gray rock underneath. Flowers and moss-covered trees and railings made the little park look cold, even on a sunny day.

Then that *smell* would meet my nose: the strong sulfur from the natural, mineral-rich waters which flowed like a little river through the entire area. Sturdy stone bridges kept the path moving across the rushing stream and small pools bubbled with the bright cloudy water as we walked the path towards the baths. I remember seeing this little tree, not much taller than me, which was trimmed to look like an umbrella. Here, we would stop and rest a moment. My mind would often get lost as I watched the people who passed by. The Old Lady often met and talked with her acquaintances, who sat and rested after a day of bathing in the mineral springs. I would stand by her side in silence, not allowed to move or do anything until she finished visiting. God forbid I had to go to the restroom, which happened from time to time. This would infuriate her as it interrupted her social time. She wouldn't let me go by myself or be out of her sight for one moment. She would have to walk with me, and angrily let me know by a poke of her cane, here and there, that I was not pleasing to her by doing this.

Private Baths

I don't know if The Old Lady paid to rent a small bath and dressing area in the spa area, but I know without a doubt this small room was "hers." We would go into this building at the top of the mountain and then into the small private bath area. I'd then help her to undress and change into a bathing suit so she could sit in the healing mineral waters. I truly believe these waters did have a healing effect upon her. She was an old woman, yet her skin was young and soft and glowed. She was a beautiful old lady, and taking care of herself in this way kept her looking young well into her nineties.

The Old Lady would spend several hours in the private baths before she'd had enough, and then I would help to dry her off and get her dressed again. "Be careful with my clothes, you stupid girl! They are never to be folded or creased," she'd scold. "You are so useless! If I hadn't taken you in, no one would have!" I would mumble politely, "Yes, Grandma," hoping to avoid a slap that might come my way.

The Waiting

When I finished dressing her and gathering her belongings, we headed back towards the park to sit. Sometimes she would visit some more. I hated the waiting: waiting for The Old Lady to finish talking; waiting for The Old Lady to finish bathing; waiting for The Old Lady to finish whatever she did. Waiting, waiting, waiting.

73

My Name is Also Freedom

I would stand and wait. I guess this might seem crazy, I mean, it was a break from sweeping or cleaning or washing, but at least my mind was free to think when I was doing those things. I was not free to think while waiting. I had to anticipate her need. If she thought for a minute that I wasn't being attentive—slap, hit, pinch, poke! I never felt more like a slave than I did while standing there, waiting to perform my next act of service!

Finally, The Old Lady would grow hungry, and we would walk down a path towards this vendor who owned a permanent stand where she would eat lunch. I loved the smell of the sticky rice he steamed in little folded packets wrapped in bamboo leaves. The Old Lady would order her meal and again I would wait, this time hoping she wouldn't be so hungry as to eat all of what was on her plate, so I might have enough of the leftovers to fill my hungry stomach as well.

I hated it when she would order fish! That meant that she would plop the chewed head or tail on top of her leftovers for me. I'd have to pick whatever pieces I could off the mangled discards and sift through the tiny bones that fell into the clumps of rice.

I can still smell the heavenly scented food freshly prepared by vendors with their carts as we traveled back towards the bus; the smell of stinky tofu, my favorite, as well as various meats on skewers and every type of steamed noodle imaginable. My stomach grumbled in vain as we continued, for I knew we wouldn't be

74

stopping to eat anything else. I carried a bag, which held some fruit and other items The Old Lady would snack on, if she felt hungry, on our long journey home.

Sadness Sets In

It's funny how difficult times color the memories we hold. It's so hard to remember those years in Taipei. I was there, but I wasn't there. I should have fond memories of things such as the Botanical Gardens in the summer time, the heady, fruity-sweet scent of the Lotus flowers blooming, the Japanese white-eyed birds darting through the trees, the red brick walls in the historic block, the fragrant incense at Longshan Temple, or the sights and sounds of the night market as we walked through the noisy, crowded street where those selling their wares called to the shoppers. I never stopped, nor was I allowed to stop, to buy anything of my own.

For those who have never been to a marketplace in Taiwan, you have missed such a feast of the senses! The streets are like a beehive, humming with activity. Every corner, every crevice, is alive with things to see, smell, and taste. During the morning, wonderful smells of cooking come from everywhere—delicious scents of soups and noodles, pastries and meats. If you weren't hungry before you began your shopping, you soon would be. Once when The Old Lady and I were shopping, she was looking for something down one of the streets, and I saw a man deep in a back corner of his shop, which was no wider than a few feet across, covered in what looked like dust. This dust covered everything! I saw him

75

roll out a huge bolt of something. He poured more "dust" on it. Then, with a large knife, he cut it into strips. When he gathered up the strips, I saw that they were noodles! The dust was flour he had sprinkled over the dough before rolling, folding, and cutting it out. I was amazed! My eyes took this all in as fast as I could, for we were not there to sightsee. Carrots, onions, greens of all kinds, papaya, pineapple, mango, and Sakya (or sugar apple) were on table after table. Displays of mushrooms and shellfish and things of all kinds were in boxes, on long tables, or on carts. Butchers set up their stands, cutting meats to size, and everywhere you looked, there was something new and different. But the smells! Those delicious smells! Sticky rice and stinky tofu! The longer we walked these streets, the more my stomach growled. I knew The Old Lady would buy and eat tasty things such as these, but I would be lucky only to eat her scraps. What places we'd visit were at her mercy—hurrying to church and then home; accompanying her on her daily walk and then home; dutifully grocery shopping and then home; waiting on her hand and foot at the spa and then home. The things that make life exciting and adventurous, full of color and pictures and smells, were held back from me. I should have those memories, yet in my mind the memories are all gray and colorless.

Someone once wrote, "Taipei has a color like the sun and the source of this color is the good days enjoyed there, a cherished childhood and brilliant golden memories."[1] I wish it had been so for me. Sadness set in. Days had become filled with heartache. My mother had told me there were to be bad days, but tomorrow had

1   Wang Zhen-xu

hope. I hoped now that what she said was true.

Taipei was growing rapidly in the 1980's. Wide, tree-lined boulevards were added along with newer apartment blocks, more stylish than our own. More upscale restaurants and cafes sprung up around the booming city. I was growing too, mostly out of my clothes once again, but as I approached my teen years, something unusual happened.

Changes

"Oh, my gosh..." I whispered to myself. I saw a stream of blood running down my leg. I was sweeping the floor at the time, so I went to the bathroom and shut the door behind me. The shorts I wore felt wet near the crotch and as I looked closer, I saw that it was blood. I had started my period and had no idea what was going on. No one ever told me anything about *anything*, certainly not about having monthly menstruation. I never saw TV or movies, I could not read a book—I had no idea when this first happened what in the world was going on. Could I be really sick? What did I do to myself?!

When The Old Lady found out, she said, "You did something bad! You filthy thing!" She was furious! She got so mad, she began to hit me. I pulled my hands up over my head as she struck me again and again. She did not explain what was happening to me. After she finished her attack, she just walked away, screaming at me to clean myself up. She never gave me pads. I had to use toilet paper. In Taiwan, we don't have rolls of toilet paper, it is more like a pack of tissues, not at all like in the U.S. I formed a pad out of a stack of tissues, but I didn't have underwear, so what could I do? My clothes were always so limited. I never had underwear, never even a bra! Usually just a few ill-fitting things that I wore until they were too tight or threadbare.

I was so desperate about what to do that I ended up using an old grocery bag to try and fashion some sort of plastic undergarment to hold the tissue. Can you believe it?! My chores and life didn't change when my period started, I just had to adapt and deal with it. The Old Lady extended neither supplies nor compassion to me.

Once, when The Old Lady and I went on her usual trek to Yangmingshan and the hot springs there, behind where she bathed, there was a place that opened to a wooded area, so as you enjoyed the mineral baths, you could also enjoy a view of nature. I began to throw the old wads of tissue from my makeshift pads out behind the trees, hoping to hide this from The Old Lady. She would never let me out of her sight, even forcing me to "hold it" for long periods of time when I had to use the restroom. When she wasn't looking, sitting in the mineral waters with her back to me, I would throw the blood-soaked tissues as far as I could. It wasn't long before the groundskeepers found them and wondered why blood-stained tissues had been thrown out there. Of course, it was only a matter of time before The Old Lady found out and questioned me about it.

"It's you, isn't it?" she confronted me one day. This was such a stressful thing for me to experience each month, not having what I needed to deal with it and not even knowing why this was happening to me, that I blurted out to her in my frustration, "Of course, it's me! What can I do? You don't give me anything—not even underwear to wear—for *this*! What am I to do? If I don't use anything, you're mad at me; I *use* something you're mad at me!" I continued like this for a minute or two, completely forgetting to control the tone I was using and too upset and angry to worry about what might happen to me. I was pretty loud when I said this to her. I think I got away with this because The Old Lady did not like to be embarrassed in front of anyone. She was afraid that someone would hear or know about her business.

Thank God, finally, some of her neighbors who had wondered why I always wore the same clothes asked her about me one day. They even asked if I had begun my period. It was these generous neighbors who donated pads and some underwear to me. God was so good!

It was so confusing to me when I would get my period. "Why does it come back, and sometimes it doesn't?" I would ask myself. I can't remember how I finally figured it out. The Old Lady felt ashamed that the neighbors had noticed this, so she began buying the pads regularly.

My Clothes

As I got older, I began to get a little bolder to ask her for clothes, mostly near Chinese New Year. This was the only time The Old Lady would give me anything.

79

My Name is Also Freedom

The bulk of my clothes were always donations, given by church members or neighbors to The Old Lady for me. Some of the donated clothes looked funny. I remember once wearing a set of clothes that were bright red and green. I looked so weird at times. Once a neighbor who sewed clothes gave some to me that were so big! I altered them myself. Clothes never fit me right.

I got shoes maybe once a year. The Old Lady would buy me shoes, but they were so cheap they had to be glued because they'd fall apart after I wore them once or twice. I got hand-me-down socks from her granddaughter, but they had holes in them. I'd try to hide the holes when I wore them by twisting them to the side or bottom of my foot. I remember this very nice couple from church. They had invited The Old Lady to visit them to have lunch. We walked to their house and knocked on the door. "Come in, come in," they said. The Old Lady took off her beautiful, expensive, handmade shoes and set them near the door. I had to take off my shoes, too. I felt so ashamed. I placed my shoes at the door and walked in with The Old Lady leaning on my arm. I was so conscious of my socks with the huge holes in them. This happened often, as The Old Lady frequently attended Bible studies at this house. I'd just fold my socks down, hoping to hide the holes.

I was always wearing the same clothes, the same socks. Her sister once gave me these bright red tennis shoes—used, of course. Another time I got a pair of bright orange ones. The Old Lady just never wanted to buy for me. I never had a bra until after I escaped. I asked her once about a bra, but she just never wanted me to look like a girl. I was growing, so I never knew my size. I wore things until they were too tight to even put on. God always provided when things got very tough, though. The neighbors were kind enough to donate, but not kind enough to say anything to others about my situation.

Abuse Continues

I helped that Old Lady do everything! I'd help her bathe, wash her back, her hair, everything. If I forgot to do something or I did anything wrong, she'd hit me or throw something at me. Often she'd say nasty things to me, sometimes loudly in public. Maybe she thought she looked powerful, and nobody would say anything to her. They let her abuse me. I was shy back then. I was very conscious of my body. It was changing, and I felt awkward about it.

"Come here, NOW!" she once demanded. I always obeyed, so I walked to her fearfully. She grabbed me, pulling my shirt over my head with one hand and holding my arm with the other, until she tore all of my clothes off. "Why are you hiding your body from me?" She pulled me, naked, towards the bathroom and then pushed me into the shower. I was humiliated! She turned the water on, and cold forceful streams hit me in the face as I lay on my back, scrambling to stand up. She threw a rag at me and told me to clean myself and the mess up. Then she just walked away.

She was so controlling in that way. I don't know if it was her plan to always treat me this way or if she was generally just a warped, unstable woman. I always felt that I had done something so

81

wrong that she was going to remind me of it, and punish me for it, every day of my life.

Whatever went on in her mind, she'd find a way to blame me somehow, some way. I was never allowed to use her shower to bathe myself. When I was allowed to take a bath, I wasn't allowed to run any water, so she'd leave her old, used water for me. I hated this! "Get a bucket and bathe," she'd demand, "You stink and are filthy!" I would have to take a little bucket I had, scoop the dirty water from the tub of her used bath water, and carry it to a shower in the back. Of course, the water wouldn't still be hot or even warm enough. It made me feel dirty to clean myself with this used water. At other times, I would use a rag to take a kind of sponge bath. But I would never let her see me do this. I was at least somewhat grateful that she was a very picky and clean old woman. She took several baths a day.

The Daughter

The Old Lady had a daughter who had moved to the United States. She was very much like her mother. She could be just as hurtful and cruel, but she was smart enough to beat me only with her words, never with her hands. She was loyal to whatever her mother decided about any matter, including when it came to me. The Daughter would visit from time to time, and at first she seemed to show me some kindness.

I was never allowed to use clean water—never, ever. And never allowed to use her shampoo or soaps. The Old Lady was so stingy and cheap with me but not on herself! She had these expensive soaps and shampoos that smelled wonderful. She insisted her daughter mail these toiletries to her from the U.S. She never used shampoo from Taiwan. When I'd help her bathe, she always kept her eye on me. She forced me to use the same detergent on my body that we used to wash the dishes. Once, she saw that the color of what I used was the same as the color of one of her fancy shampoos. She had a fit! Flying into a rage, she accused me of taking her precious shampoo from America. "You thief!" she called me. For three days, she yelled at me, and she told all her friends that I had stolen her shampoo, just because the color of the dish soap—green I think it was—was the same as her shampoo. "Can you believe what this ungrateful granddaughter of mine did?" she would begin when the ladies from church would come over for tea. I had to stand there, cringing inside, while she went off on how horrible I was. I didn't even do it! She continued to condemn me long after everyone left. "You are my slave. How can you use my stuff?! You are a slave, you will never be on my same level. You cannot use the same stuff as me, you cannot eat with me!" After that, I was forced to use laundry soap, this washing powder, on my body and hair. It was so rough, and it irritated my skin and hair. This was so very hurtful for me. I felt so worthless.

Chapter 7

Truth and Lies

There are several different religions in Taiwan. My mother believes in God, the Christian God. I was amazed that The Old Lady followed the Christian faith. I would see her reading her Bible but then all of a sudden scream hurtful things at me. Then, like nothing had happened, she would just go back to reading that Holy Book. This was so hard to understand.

The Old Lady, however, was diligent about attending church. She never missed a service! Of course, I went everywhere she went, and church was no exception.

Every Thursday there was a woman's Bible study. We would walk there. The Old Lady loved to walk! Since the Bible study was from two to four in the afternoon, we would get back to the house just in time for me make dinner.

My Name is Also Freedom

The church was small. They wore robes on the stage, and everyone sang. Halfway through the service, they would take communion. The Old Lady wouldn't let me participate because I had never been baptized in that church. "You cannot do this with us. You are not a part of this church," she'd say. "You have not been baptized."

The Old Lady was always afraid of anyone getting too close to me. I think she knew that if people talked to me they would find out that I was her slave. The pastor knew something wasn't right with me and the family, but like others in the church, they felt it wasn't any of their business.

Donations

My choice of church clothes was pretty limited. I did have this cream-colored dress; it was long with lace and a red stripe. It was made of a thin material, so you could see through it. I had no underwear, so I wore shorts underneath it. I wore it every Sunday. People would ask The Old Lady why I wore the same dress over and over again. She'd lie and say, "It's her favorite dress, this is why she always wears it; she won't wear anything else to church." It wasn't true of course; I had nothing else to wear. To keep it clean and from getting worn out, I only wore it to church. Later, I had some grey pants. They were actually black, but I bleached them so people would think they were a different pair of pants. She'd then say, "Those are her favorite pants; that is why she always wears them." Others would ask me, "Why do you always wear that all the time? How come you never change your clothes?" So I would take turns with what I had. That was the beginning of church people donating clothes to me on a regular basis. One lady from church gave me a sweater. It was so nice of her. It was so soft. I wore it all the time. I was grateful for everything given to me, no matter the color or if it fit me properly.

Loving Church

I truly loved the days we went to church. This was the place that I could sleep! Because I was always up so late with The Old Lady and working so hard all day, I was exhausted! I also knew she wouldn't dare hit or pinch me in church for fear of what others might think. I felt safe and looked forward to this haven twice a week. In addition to the Thursday Bible study, we attended Sunday services. I loved to listen to the preacher's messages! I would carefully sit in such a way that was comfortable enough to drift in and out of slumber, listening to God's Word, without looking like I was asleep. I especially loved when the pastor began to read this part about love, it was like he meant the words for me. He read, "Love is patient, love is kind. It does not envy, it does not boast, it is not proud. It does not dishonor others, it is not self-seeking, it is not easily angered, it keeps no record of wrongs. Love does not delight in evil but rejoices with the truth. It always protects, always trusts, always hopes, always perseveres. Love never fails." I thought about these words. "Love is patient, love is kind." That passage is my favorite!

Getting Baptized

The woman behind me in church one day said, "Take one," as she passed a communion cracker to me. I knew The Old Lady would not like this. "No, she cannot," I said. The Old Lady explained to the woman, "She has not been baptized." It was not too long after this that the pastor met with The Old Lady. He kept pestering her to have me baptized. "God loves her, and you come to church all the time, why not let her be baptized? This church is like a family," he said. He told her the next baptism was scheduled for around Christmas time. She finally agreed. She was mad, but because of her fear of anyone finding out about me, she let the pastor do this. So that December I was baptized in a swimming pool. I remember how cold the water was! I went down into the water as The Old Lady just sat there. The service lasted about an hour, and they even gave me a certificate. The Old Lady was not happy about it. We stopped attending that church soon after that.

Believing

"Clean out all of this trash," The Old Lady said. "All these useless things from my son's business must be thrown in the trash." She left me in one of the upstairs rooms with a broom and dust bin. I picked up old magazines and catalogues and tossed them in the can. As I was doing this, I came across a picture of Jesus. It had been torn out of some book or something and it lay there in the bits of dust and dirt. I carefully picked it up and brushed it off. "I have a place for you," I said to the Savior, who had his arms open wide and a heart painted between his robes. At that time, I slept in a little crawlspace where odds and ends were stored. It was only about as wide as my body. I could touch the walls when I lay there. Mice would often run across my chest as I slept at night. I put the picture in my pocket and finished my work. Later that night when I went to lie down, I placed the picture against the wall, fastening it with a piece of tape. "Good night, God," I said. "I know You will help me." This was my altar. I would tell my troubles to Jesus and pray for His help. I believed He hadn't forgotten about me. I believed He would help me.

When I shared my story much later on, I mentioned that The Old Lady followed Christian beliefs, religiously reading her Bible and attending church regularly. So many people were shocked when they heard this; they couldn't understand why she did what she did. How in the world could she treat me in such a way if she was a Christian?

My answer was simple. I told them, "When I went to church with The Old Lady, I listened to God's Words and believed what the pastor said, but The Old Lady—she did not."

Chapter 8

My Father is Dead

I can't say that there was *a moment* that God spoke to me for the first time. I really feel that He has always been with me. When I would cry myself to sleep at night, wondering why my mother never came back for me like she promised, He would remind me of what my mother had told me, "Today was a bad day, but tomorrow will be better; rest your head and sleep." I knew somehow God was there; that He would someday give me a better day if I could just hang on. I never hated God in all my troubles, but there were moments I was so very angry with Him. I would vent at God, "Why do You not see? That Old Lady sits in her chair, her Bible open, her lips forming words from what You have written in there, and then she screams and yells such terrible things about me! She believes in You? I don't understand."

There was always this voice behind me, "You know it is

not right she treats you this way; it was not right for your parents to have sold you," but I never found peace listening to that voice. When I let that attitude stay, I was miserable. I was led by these questions: Do I feel good? Do I feel peace?

Deep inside, I knew it wasn't God who did this to me; I knew the Bible said to do good things, like love, for I had heard what was written on those pages myself as I sat in church with her, week after week. She might read those words and tell herself she knows the God who wrote them, but His words were words of love and kindness and forgiveness, things she never showed towards me, even though I called her Grandma.

The Call

"You can't have more money, if that's what her father is thinking. I won't do it! I paid over $10,000 NTD, and for what?! A scrawny, useless girl who is more trouble at times than she is worth?! If that's not why you called, then what do you want?!" I heard the heated words as I was in the bedroom making The Old Lady's bed and tidying her room. I was curious as to who she was talking to, but I had learned to mind my own business and never ask questions. I tugged at my shirt that was now so short on me that my skin showed just above my hips. My pants were becoming so tight that just bending to smooth out the blankets caused them to pull on me, shorting my reach, but I was grateful that there were no holes in them—at least not yet.

My Father is Dead

"What do you want me to do about it? I cannot spare to let her go for any length of time. Who will do all the work that needs to be done?!" the conversation continued. The Old Lady was clearly upset about something, and I was pretty sure that something had to do with me. Suddenly, the shouting stopped, and I heard The Old Lady's footsteps stomping towards the bedroom.

The News

"Your father is dead," The Old Lady blurted out, unemotionally. "Your family has called to request you be sent to attend the funeral, but you will not stay the required time. I will not have you gone for more than the day of the funeral," she went on in an angry tone. "I cannot go with you, so I will send someone with you." She turned and walked out of the room. I stood there, hit by this news. This was July of 1994. I was about fourteen years old. I hadn't seen my dad since he had driven me to Taipei to live with The Old Lady, promising me he would return. That was over seven years ago, and I was angry with him, then and now, to be left with this horrible lady. But he *was* my father, and he was dead. I never had the chance to tell him about my anger, to reason with him to be brought back home, to cry and beg him to bring me to my mother. I started to remember that last day with my family. Tears began to fill my eyes, but I could not let The Old Lady see them.

The Phone Calls

I had had no idea that The Old Lady had kept in touch with my family. I knew my father had called a few times because The Old

My Name is Also Freedom

Lady would put me on the phone with him. Like some kidnapped victim, I was only allowed to say, "Hello, Father," then she would take the phone away from me. She would tell me later that my dad was calling only to ask for more money, but I didn't believe her. Once, when she handed me the phone, I was able to quickly say, "Hello, Father ... please, I want to come home," but then she snatched the receiver out of my hand and shouted at me to leave the room.

I guess she had also written to my family from time to time all those years, sending them pictures of me and letting them know that I was okay and that I "loved" my life with her. She told them lies, like that I never wanted to see them again. I had no idea that they had also contacted her, hoping to see me or reconnect in some way. She had never shown me any letters, never told me about any of *those* calls, and of course she never told me that they had known all along where I was. I believed her when she'd said they didn't want me and had never tried to come see me. Why shouldn't I believe her? Selling me to her was a fact. And besides, they promised to come and bring me home. They had broken that promise.

The Funeral

I could not travel to my father's funeral alone. The Old Lady would not allow that! Her son's girlfriend would go with me, making sure to keep me in tow, and bring me home as soon as possible. I didn't have the proper clothes for a funeral, and of course, none would be given to me, so I went with what I had. The girlfriend called for

My Father is Dead

a taxi to take us to the train station and we made the long journey back towards my home village. The Old Lady's lies about my family filled me with doubts about them. "They sold you. If you go back, they will just sell you again," she had said one day. This was true. They *did* sell me. Although those first days and months I had missed them so much, time had brought anger and hate to me and I often battled them both at night as I lay on the cold hard floor, with my head on my pillow of smelly rags, thinking about home. Sometimes I imagined myself shouting at my parents, pronouncing judgement on the terrible thing they did by selling me. I wished, at times, for awful things to happen to them, only regretting it all as I finally fell asleep. I never had love for my father. Now he was dead. My heart was torn inside. He was my father, after all.

My dad, who was an alcoholic, had been killed in an accident. One morning he had been drinking heavily, got on his motorcycle to drive home and lost control. His motorcycle spun around out of control and smashed into a wall. It was a very bad accident. I remembered my dad's temper, his rash ways of dealing with circumstances in life. I remember how he treated my mother. I thought of my mother and sisters. Tears fell down my face as I looked out the window of the train, and we came closer to our stop.

I was not allowed to get too close to my family at the funeral. Everyone was crying as I stood there, like a bystander. The moment did not seem real. The details are so hard to remember, so hazy. I knew my family was upset that I would not stay for the seven days our culture required, but how could I tell them that the son's girlfriend was there to watch me, and I couldn't stay? The Old Lady would find out, and it would be bad for me. We stayed just a few hours before the girlfriend forced me to leave. I can still see my sisters crying, my mother standing there. I was so guarded and un-trusting of them. It kept me from reaching out to them; telling them what had happened to me. Sometimes I wish I could go back and do things differently, but I can't. We took a taxi from there, stayed the night not far from the village, and then headed back to Taipei early the next morning. I would not see any of my family again for another eighteen years.

Part III
America

Chapter 9

Trip to America

The Old Lady's Daughter had lived in the United States for many years. She had married an American and done pretty well for herself. They owned several businesses and had property. I remember when I was much younger, The Old Lady went to stay with her daughter for several months in the U.S. while I stayed with The Old Lady's sister. I was always kept by someone. She never left me alone. In 2000, however, I travelled to the U.S. with The Old Lady on what was supposed to be a six-month visit. I, of course, cooked and cleaned and waited on the woman hand and foot; it wasn't a vacation for me. She always introduced me to others as a grand-daughter. That is how she avoided questions, and I was able move so freely and travel with this family. I guess this could have been an adventure for me as well, but it turned into a nightmare!

This was the first time I had ever left Taiwan. The trip

quickly took a horribly wrong turn when I suddenly became extremely sick. It must've been the dry air or change in humidity that
brought it all on. The weather just seemed to affect me badly. My
skin became very dry and cracked. It felt itchy, and a rash covered
my entire body; my legs were the most affected. This was extremely
painful, and soon open sores began to form where the dry, irritated skin had split open. I suppose it was an act of kindness on The
Daughter's part to give me some lotion to put on it. But even the
acts of kindness were tainted with selfish cruelties. The lotion was
old and expired. I twisted off the lid, and my nose caught a faint,
unpleasant smell. What could I do? My legs were in excruciating
pain, and this was all I had. I squeezed a small dab of the lotion into
my palm and carefully rubbed it into my wounds. It stung a little,
but I continued putting it on my legs until I covered every dry and
cracked patch. The next morning my legs felt hot and tight, and
when I turned up my pant legs, I saw a reddish ring forming around
the edges of the sores. I put more lotion on. I did this for over two
and a half weeks until the lotion was gone. My legs only grew worse.
They were now not only still red, but swollen. It got so bad, I could
barely pull my pants on, and my skin oozed a clear, sticky liquid.

Something is Wrong

Each day, the pain grew worse until I could hardly walk. Sitting was
almost impossible. My chores did not change. I still had to get up
at 5 a.m. to cook and clean and take care of the family. I did this
slower than usual and without sympathy, just disapproving glares.
One morning, as I led The Old Lady on her early morning walk

to the park, a neighbor called to us as we walked past her, "Your granddaughter ... her legs ... why are her pants so wet and her legs so swollen?! Show me your legs, young lady." The woman was watching us as she watered her lawn. She often chatted to The Old Lady as we passed her house. "It's best to water before the sun gets too hot. A good time to walk as well," she'd say. It was not idle chit chat today. The Old Lady could not avoid her, she had to stop. I was wearing these purple pants and walking rather stiff legged because of the pain. The sores were oozing the clear fluid, wet and sticky, visible through my pants, which were now wet and clinging to my legs. I carefully peeled my pant legs up to show the woman my swollen and infected legs. She gasped at the sight and blurted out, "You need to take her to the doctor right away!" I could sense the anger rising in The Old Lady. Her embarrassment that someone had noticed me made her furious. The Old Lady made up some excuse, her words stuttering as they came out of her mouth. She made no real sense and mumbled a final, "Yes, she will see my doctor very soon," to the woman, and we hurriedly turned around and headed back to the house.

We were barely inside when The Old Lady unleashed a wave of insults, "What is wrong with you?! Why have you let this happen?! Now I will have to take you to see my doctor. How will you pay for this? You don't have any money. You will not be able to pay me, you lazy girl!" she ranted, "See, I told you that you were trouble, always causing trouble. You are lucky that I ever took you in! No one wants you, no one will ever want you!" The words she spoke dug deep into my heart, wounding me much worse than the oozing, weeping sores on my legs. I ran off to the bathroom, closed the door, and cried.

The Doctor

A few days later, we were able to get in to see the doctor. Both The Old Lady and I went into the examination room and waited. After some time, the doctor came in. The Old Lady spoke for me as the doctor told me to roll up my pant legs. I wore the same purple pants, I had no others at the time. When he saw my condition, he was scared to even touch my legs. "Oh my gosh!" he said, thinking my terrible rash might be contagious. He studied my legs, trying hard not to get too close or to touch them.

After a few moments he asked, "Were you using anything, soap maybe, that could have caused this? Stop using whatever you may be putting on them immediately." I told him how itchy my legs were and about the lotion The Daughter had given me and what had happened. He listened, never taking his eyes off of my legs, nodding his head. He opened a drawer and pulled out a syringe, placing a large needle on the top. "This should help somewhat … " his voice trailed off. He gave me the shot and a prescription for more antibiotics. I didn't have insurance or money to pay him, so The Old Lady was forced to pay. Although she complained under her breathe, she paid him. Firmly she asked, "What about travel? We have just a few more weeks, and then we must return to Taiwan." A look of concern fell over his face. He was worried about me.

"She needs rest. I will need to see her again to make sure she is healing up properly. She cannot travel until then," he turned away and scribbled the prescription on a pad of paper. I felt relieved. I knew that my daily workload would not change, and rest was unlikely, but finally my body would begin to heal. I took in a deep breath and let it out slowly. I slowly pulled my pant legs down and slid off the cold metal table.

I could feel The Old Lady's anger, even though she didn't say a word on the bus the ride home. Wheels were turning in The Old Lady's mind. She would arrange for her daughter to change my travel visa to be extended another six months. It was a long six months before we returned to Taiwan. I eventually healed, but I still have scars on my legs.

My father's grave site

My first pair of shoes Judy bought me.

Dawu Township

First time I went to see my family again when I was free.

Chapter 10

Leaving Taiwan

I had begun to notice subtle changes in The Old Lady. She had always been mean towards me, but her actions became more and more bizarre. I was used to doing a chore and having her be displeased. This was my life. I was never good enough for her. I remember a woman visited once who had also been a servant of hers before I had come along. The Old Lady was so sweet to her, recounting memories of her service with fondness. All the while I stood there, waiting for a command, hearing her compare me to this woman. "And *this* one!" she shot a glance my way. "So useless! Much too little and incompetent!" They continued to visit, drinking tea and laughing from time to time. When the visitor had left, I began to clear away the dishes to wash them. The Old Lady walked over to me.

"Did you enjoy eavesdropping on us, thief?" She reached

out her hand and grabbed my breast, right at the nipple, and pinched it as hard as she could with her fingers. I winched in pain and dropped a small plate that contained scraps of pastry left over from tea. The plate fell to the floor and broke into pieces. "You lazy, careless child!" she screamed and slapped me across the face. "You won't eat those scraps now as your lunch. Throw them in the trash, and I will check to make sure they stay there!" I rubbed my breast as I knelt on the ground, picking up the pieces of the broken plate and pastry crumbs that were scattered on the floor. The Old Lady had never pinched me like this before, but it began to happen more and more often. Her suspicions of me grew, and her behavior became extremely erratic. I wasn't sure how old she was, but I knew she must be in her late eighties. Things seemed to get worse as she got older. She began to kick me and accuse me of ridiculous things. She was becoming crazy and her violent outbursts became more frequent.

"Please, Grandma ... Don't!"

"This pot had *plenty* of tea left in it. That thieving girl!" The Old Lady shouted from the kitchen. My heart jumped at those words. I was clearing away the rest of the dishes from the table after all of her guests had left. They had enjoyed a wonderful lunch of chicken, sticky rice balls, and tea as I stood serving or waiting to serve just like I always did. I knew she would probably slap me, but I fearfully walked into the kitchen to face The Old Lady's anger.

"Grandma, what is wrong? I did not drink any of your tea. You saw me the whole time your friends were here. When could

108

Leaving Taiwan

I have done this? I did not. I wouldn't steal your tea!" My voice cracked as I knew there would be some punishment, but I didn't expect what happened next.

"I will not stand for this from a slave like you!" she screamed. Her eyes seethed with such rage that I was taken by surprise for a brief moment. Suddenly, she grabbed me by the hair and pulled me so hard I fell to the ground. I was caught off guard and scrambled to get up, but I couldn't. She held on tight and continued to yank and twist my hair so violently that I flopped back and forth on the floor. Her strength in doing this was beyond what I was used to and I didn't know what to do but cry, "Please, Grandma! I swear I didn't drink your tea! How could I? Please, please, don't hurt me like this...ahhh ... please! My neck! Ouch ... Grandma!"

I begged and begged her to stop, but she was like a machine. Her grip tightened, and she began to drag me down the hall. I reached up, trying to pull her fingers off of my hair, but it was impossible. I slid on the tile, but when she reached the carpet, she grabbed me with both hands and pulled even harder, pulling me forcefully further down the hall. My dress bunched up around my waist, and my bare bottom scraped against the course fibers and burned as it tore my skin. I screamed out in pain as The Old Lady yanked me into the bathroom. I collapsed in a heap, my arm hitting the base of the toilet. Oh, how I hurt all over! Thinking this horrible scene was done, I sat up. That is when The Old Lady jerked the brush used to clean the toilet from its stand and began to shove it into my mouth! I grit my teeth to keep it out, but she rubbed my lips raw with the harsh bristles of the brush. "That will teach you to take what is not yours!" she hissed. She now had one hand on my shirt trying to force my face back towards the filthy toilet brush. She shoved it again and again at my mouth until she was satisfied and then pushed me down and threw the brush at my head. "And clean this mess up or I'll make things worse for you!" she commanded, as she stomped back down the hall towards the kitchen.

A small drop of blood dripped down my chin; one of the bristles had punctured the inside of my lower lip. I sobbed as I sat there. I was in such pain that it took a long time for me to stand up. When I did, I looked in the mirror, and I rinsed my mouth out carefully. My cheeks were puffy and my eyes red from crying so hard. My face was scratched and bleeding. My throat felt sore. It must've been from my screams, begging her to stop. I peeled my skirt up to see the raw spot where the rug had burned me. I dabbed it with a piece of wet tissue. My head was so sore, and my neck ached. I couldn't turn it without a stabbing pain on either side. But it was inside where I hurt the most. This woman, this grandma of mine, hated me so. Why did she hate me? Why couldn't I please her? I wanted her to love me so very badly. She was the only family I had. I knew I had to clean up the mess in the bathroom, but I cried and cried the whole time.

Moving to the U.S.

I was about seventeen years old when The Old Lady told me, "We are going to live in the United States. My daughter wants me to come. You will come live with us to take care of me. Things will not change for you; you are a slave and will always be a slave," she said, pounding her authoritative words into me. The Old Lady's daughter was concerned now that her mother was getting older. She wanted me to continue to take care of her but live in the U.S. with The Daughter and her husband. My previous trip there was not a good experience, so I was afraid. I didn't have any travel papers or anything, so somehow this family was going to get me there. I don't remember how much longer we stayed in Taiwan after this, maybe a year or so, but I remember wondering if my family knew where I was now, and that I was going to be living in the U.S.

The Daughter had come to Taiwan several times in order to arrange all the travel plans, taking me to sign papers, having pictures of me taken, and many things which I cannot now recall. The Old Lady and her daughter always made sure things looked perfect. I always presented myself as being happy and willing to anyone who would question me or suggest otherwise. Did I have a choice? Was this the life I had chosen? I just did what they wanted. What could I do? I was never to say no, ever. When things were all in place, it was time to start boxing things up. The building belonged to The Old Lady's son, so most of The Old Lady's possessions could be boxed up and stored there, but she wanted to go through her things and decide what she thought was necessary to bring with her to her new home in the states.

Packing
I helped The Old Lady pack while movers took care of any other possessions she planned on taking. The Old Lady trusted my skills

in picking out her outfits—it was the one thing she didn't criticize me for—so I chose a few of her favorites and placed them carefully in her suitcase. I thought about what I owned that would go with me. I had no clothes to speak of and was never allowed to buy anything for myself, but I did have a Bible. A church member had given it to me as a gift. "This book contains the very words of God. He spoke them to us all, and it still speaks to us, if we just listen," the kind Christian explained. I looked at the worn, black leather cover. Two gold-colored words were written across the front. Although I couldn't read it, I promised myself, one day, I would read this book. "Thank you so much," I had said as I bowed slightly, holding my new treasure. This was my only possession. I would keep this with me.

Becoming Sharon

When everything was packed up, and the movers had taken what things The Old Lady wanted, The Daughter turned to me with a stern look and said, "You say nothing at the airport, at customs, you hear me? You will nod and only agree with what I or my mother say, understand?" She grabbed my shoulders tightly as she said, "Understand?" I knew this was important, and I was not to disobey her or things would be very bad for me. The Daughter's words were always so cutting and poisonous to me, but she never touched or hurt me like The Old Lady did. "You are now to be called Sharon. This is now your name—SHARON. We will be living as Americans now." I felt her firm grip and knew I was to go along *with everything*. I had been with this family since I was seven years old. Yes, I was a slave, they had bought me, but I was also a part of their family. It was a terrible, abusive family, but I was a part of it. Where could I go if I left? What would happen if I spoke up? The fear and inability to know what I could do kept me in this place.

So I came to live in the U.S. It was such a big place! Where Taipei was busy with motorcycles, buses, and people crammed everywhere, the U.S. was more spread out. There were still buses, people, and cars—so many cars—but the streets were huge! The neighborhoods were so much different than where I had lived. The house I lived in here with The Old Lady and her daughter was nice. Carpet was on all the floors, and they had a backyard with grass and trees and flowers. The weather was much drier, and I remembered what had happened on my first trip.

Maybe things will be better here, I thought.

The Workload Gets Heavier

When I lived with The Old Lady in Taiwan, I did all of the work. I cleaned her very large apartment building. She forced me to mop, scrub, cook, clean, wash dishes, mend clothes, and do laundry. I took care of her personally as well, making her tea, bathing her, dressing her, cooking for her and her son. I'd help her do her daily exercises, and routinely make the journey to Yangmingshan, where I waited on her hand and foot. I would end my days, exhausted, finally allowed to sleep after massaging The Old Lady's feet and hands. Here in the U.S., I was expected to take care of The Old Lady, the house, AND The Old Lady's Daughter and her husband! I still awoke every morning at five, but they expected me to adjust all of my chores to the schedule of the rest of the household. Things got worse when they decided that I would go to work with The Daughter and help run her store. "My mother will go with us to the store, and you will come to look after her," The Daughter had said. But most of the time, The Old Lady went into a back room to watch TV while I cleaned the store. I would sweep, vacuum, clean the bathroom, take out the trash, set up and put away items in the shop, and do whatever errands The Daughter told me to do. As soon as we got home in the evenings, which would be 6 p.m. or later, I hurried to cook them all dinner and then tend to The Old Lady's needs again, going to sleep almost regularly at 1 a.m. The Old Lady had a large bed, but she required me to sleep on the floor in her room, in case she needed help in the middle of the night.

Most seventeen-year-old girls are giggly and so happy in life. They have boyfriends, hang out with friends, maybe stay long after school to do cheerleading or participate in some sport or club. Not me. I felt old and tired. I got only little glimpses of what girls my age did, but I knew how they looked and dressed when The Daughter's son's girlfriend, Kim, would come over. I noticed everything about her—how she dressed and what make-up she wore.

I was careful not to let The Daughter catch me looking too long at anything. She watched me like a hawk and used any excuse to humiliate me and tear me down. "You like Kim's cute skirt, huh?" she said slyly one day after she saw me looking at her. "You can't wear that skirt, you know. Your butt is so big! I am ashamed even to have you out front in my shop, you ugly thing! You are chasing customers away with the way you look." She continued her cutting comments with a nasty look on her face. "You can't even speak English. What is wrong with you, you stupid girl? No one will ever find a use for you."

Every day was filled with work to do. I never got a day off or even a moment to rest. Sundays were especially hard because by then I was so tired from the week and the family expected me to serve them on their day off! They didn't want to do anything for themselves, especially on Sunday.

My Only Friend

"Pick up these dog messes in the backyard now!" demanded The Daughter early one Sunday morning. "My mother will want to get to church on time so you had better get it done, you lazy girl!" I had just finished cooking breakfast for The Daughter and her husband and had started on cleaning up the dishes. "Uhhhh—" I whispered, as I set the towel down and hurried to the sliding glass door.

The family had a little backyard with flowers in it. The Daughter's son had this really big dog, and she let him keep it there in the backyard. After breakfast every morning, I would usually pick up dog messes, water the plants, and do any needed gardening. The backyard was the only place I could be alone with my thoughts. I would try to look busy outside, so I could think. *How long until this is all over?* I'd wonder. *I want to be free.* I would wish for someone to take care of me. I had lots of wishes: I wanted to go to school, to go out and have fun like normal people. I would imagine

115

that this family would change and treat me better, like a real family. Every day, I wished my life was better, and that I could feel pretty. Out of all of the chores I did—the only one that I liked was playing with the dog and feeding him. All other chores I did like a robot. I had to do them. But I loved that dog. He liked me, too. He was my best friend, for he listened to me talk about all my troubles.

As I started to unlock the door, I glanced down at all the shoes lined up in pairs just on the other side of it. I noticed one of The Daughter's shoes was missing. "Here boy, come, come on boy," I called, looking for the big, beautiful Husky. Although I loved this huge gentle giant of a dog, so often I had to cover up for his behavior. He liked to steal a shoe or two when he could and chew them up. He'd taken one of The Old Lady's shoes once and of course, I was yelled at as much as the dog was for taking it. Today, I was sure he'd gotten hold of The Daughter's sandal. "Here boy," I called again. I walked towards the shovel, searching for his messes as I did. He was such a good dog. As much as he loved chewing shoes, he never stole mine. Once, The Old Lady commented, "Why does he never chew your sandals?" Everyone in that house had had a shoe torn up by him—but not me! I was so thankful because I only had one pair of shoes. How he knew this, I didn't know. If he'd chewed mine, I'd have to wear them just as they were.

He's Gone!

I picked up the shovel, carefully scooped up a rather large doggie mess, and headed to the bucket which I had lined with a trash bag. After I put the lid on the bucket, I noticed the gate on the side of the yard was open, and the dog was missing! I hurriedly looked all over the yard calling his name, but he was gone. I ran towards the house to grab some dog treats and the leash, hoping to coax the dog to come to me, if I found him. He would often escape, running out the side gate if it wasn't latched tight. I would get blamed because I would take the trash cans out that gate once a week. I couldn't go after him because I wasn't allowed to walk the dog alone, or even be out front without permission. But on this day, I dashed out into the side yard anyway and ran towards the front of the house. Where could he be? Down towards the end of the street, sniffing a large bush with great interest, was the dog! Relieved, yet still a bit nervous he might run, I called to him sweetly, "Come, baby, come to me." I continued to repeat this as I walked slowly and calmly towards him. "I have a doggie treat for you," I said. "A crunchy treat. Mmm. Taste good," I coaxed. He turned his head and walked over to me. He sniffed the treat and began munching the biscuit, covering my hand in drool. I carefully clicked his leash onto his collar. Suddenly, he pulled away and nearly dragged me down on the sidewalk! I had to pull him as hard as I could, for he did NOT want to come back home with me. He was so heavy and strong, but somehow I was able to get him back in the yard before anyone knew he was missing.

The Daughter

I continued to cook for the family. They would eat first, and I would eat last. They gave me whatever was left over. They gave the dog more food than I got. They treated me worse than a dog! I never drank much milk. I made it by mixing it from a powder in those days. The Daughter's son liked milk with his oatmeal. Every morning, I made oatmeal for him. If I accidentally spilled any of it while cooking, I would scoop it up and taste it. The Daughter would always say to me, "Do not steal my son's food." Whether I did or not, she would still scold or punish me. I would cry at some point every day because of what one of them said or did to me. Once in a while, The Daughter would cook eggs for her son and give me the yolks. She would say, "Here, eat it," and I would eat it because I was so hungry. Even if food had been in the fridge, and it turned sour, I still would eat it. Today, I can't stand to eat just the yolks, I'll only eat scrambled eggs.

New Clothes

I do remember once asking for some new clothes or some money to get some. I was never given anything special. I continued to wear the same clothes day after day. I once wore the same pair of shoes for three years, they were these open-toed type of sandals. I never even knew my own shoe size, so I was excited when one day The Daughter said yes.

She took me to a discount store and said I could choose something under five dollars. I was actually able to find a few things, but when I began to wear them, she made fun of me. "Oh, you think you look so pretty in your new clothes, do you?" The Daughter said one day in that jealous-sounding voice she had. "Wanting men to pay attention to you, eh? Are you going to flirt to get a boyfriend with your new clothes?" I felt guilty for having something nice. I felt ashamed. I didn't know that what they said was wrong. I thought they must be right, or why would they say those things?

Alone in America

They *never* allowed me to have close relationships with anyone, fearing I would find the courage to escape or that others might discover the truth, so I was *never* left alone. They were always with me. I had thought about escaping, but how could I? I didn't know where to go. If they catch me, I thought, it will be worse! After many months of being in America, The Daughter needed more and more help at her work. I didn't speak any English, and this was beginning to be a problem.

"I want you to spend time on this computer to learn English," she told me one day. "There is this program where you can learn. You just put a CD in here," she motioned to the box (hard drive, she told me), "and it will come up on the screen. Do this when you are finished with your chores." Finished with my chores? When am I ever finished with my chores? Most of the time, I'd be half asleep and doing a chore, or I would be doing one for The Old Lady, and The Daughter would interrupt me and ask me to do one for her. I was forever doing chores, and now I would have to find time to do this? Once or twice, well after midnight, I'd try to study English this way, but it was not very often.

Being in America and living in a large house, I had hoped I would have a bed to sleep in. The Old Lady had had an extra room with a bed in it back in Taiwan, but she had still forced me to sleep on the floor. Maybe here things would be different.

At first The Old Lady did tell me, "Come sleep in the bed." Maybe it was because she was so old and got cold at night, I don't know, but I welcomed those times. When The Daughter saw this, she would not allow it. Once, The Daughter came into her mother's bedroom for some reason and saw her mother was not in the bed, but I was. She questioned me. "Little sister," she scolded in Chinese, "Why do you not help her? She is in the bathroom alone without help. Now you must always sleep on the floor!" From then on, if The Old Lady got up to use the bathroom, I would have to get up too because she would step on me when getting out of bed.

The Forever Lie

The family continued to hide my identity. If anyone asked who I was, they would say that I was their granddaughter or their God-daughter, depending on who I was with. My life was a lie. They made up everything. No one wanted to get involved, so people would never question why I was with them or who I really was. The family kept everyone distant from me. If I accepted food that church members offered me at a potluck or event, they would slap me later. "Why you waste this food? You are fed at home!" they told me.

The Daughter's husband, who was American, once saw that I was sad. He asked me, "Why are you crying, Sharon?" He knew, of course, what was going on, but he never said anything. He knew I was a slave. He saw how they treated me. I didn't answer him, but later The Daughter found out he had spoken to me. She came storming down from upstairs and confronted me, "You are so evil; you threaten our marriage, you whore! I know you are trying to seduce my husband!" she accused me. She would say horrible things to me in Chinese and then end by saying, "It doesn't matter what you wear or how you dress. You are a slave; you will always be a slave." I hated her when she said this, but I just sat there crying. I had no fight in me. I was empty inside.

Dreaded Shopping

I hated to go shopping with The Daughter. I couldn't read English at all, so finding the exact items she wanted always ended up with her shouting at me, "Are you stupid! You can't figure anything out on your own?" The Daughter became more verbally abusive as time went on. I think The Old Lady started that. I overheard her talking with her daughter saying, "I believe Sharon is flirting with your husband." Why The Old Lady said these things, I don't know. Was it on purpose to create problems for me, or was she getting so senile and paranoid that she truly believed this about me? I don't know, but The Daughter's horrid comments to me cut me deeply.

There were times at the shop when it was so busy that they would allow me to pick up lunch for The Old Lady and her daughter. They would call the order in, and I walked (just a few doors down from where we worked) to the restaurant to pick it up. They never allowed me to order a lunch for myself. I ate what The Old Lady did not finish. I hated how she always placed her chewed leftovers on top of any untouched food. She did this on purpose, so I would have to pick up the discards—bones, skin, half-bitten pieces, spat-out fatty chunks—in order to eat any untouched rice or noodles underneath. I HATED THIS.

I was doing more and more work at the shop, working with customers or standing out front to bring customers in. I know people witnessed this family's cruelty, for The Old Lady had trouble hiding it at the store. Once, when she was mad about something, she grabbed her cane and hit me on the back of the legs. She hit me so hard, I nearly fell over. Several people turned to see what had happened, but nobody said a word. It only made these women more bold in their cruel behavior towards me. The Daughter now berated me more publicly without shame. Other shop owners overheard her saying, "You, dumb, stupid girl! No wonder you're only a servant." They saw me crying many times. But they were too scared to come forward. They stayed silent, and I stayed a slave.

Chapter 11

Unexpected Friendship

It had now become a regular task for me to go with the Old Lady and her daughter to help out at her business. I would clean the restrooms, sweep, vacuum, and do whatever she needed before the shop opened. Like most of the work I did, it began in the early morning hours, long before the sun was up. I lived in a constant state of exhaustion, working eighteen to twenty hours a day! I had become numb to the routine chores. I did them mechanically, my body going through the motions, my heart and head someplace else. I got up and dressed in the same tattered outfit I always wore and after serving my captors' needs, I would get listlessly into the car.

We would arrive at the shop just before 6 a.m., and The Daughter would hurriedly push me towards the open shop door. "You, go clean the workshop and toilets before the men arrive.

My Name is Also Freedom

Sweep and get rid of the trash. Hurry! Customers will come." I
gathered my cleaning supplies together and trudged toward the
workshop. The workshop was a long, narrow room that contained a
telephone, restrooms, and a small workbench and chair. If something needed to be repaired, it could be done there. It was cramped
and dusty and dark. It had no windows to see in or out of, and the
door could be locked from the inside. I began my daily chores here,
cleaning the room and dumping the trash. The restrooms were
always filthy. They were the only ones in the building, and everyone
used them. I finished the sweeping and carted my supplies into the
men's room and began scrubbing the toilets. So often I felt like I
was dead and yet alive at the same time. Did I hate scouring these
disgusting toilets more than mopping the floors? I felt nothing. I
could feel my heart beating, but I cleaned like I was dead; uncaring
what the chore was or how long it would take. Why should I care?
That would not change anything. Every day was filled with burdens
that would be repeated tomorrow. Maybe today would have a little
less trouble. I could at least feel some measure of hope in that.

When I finished with the workroom and toilets, I would
start on the rest of the building: vacuuming, dusting, cleaning. I
had been doing this now for quite some time, day after day, month
after month, and no one who came in ever asked me, "Who are you,
and why do you do this?" When the tenants who rented out the
sections of the shop set up their wares, they looked at me quiz-
zically, but never said a word. I saw in their eyes they knew that
something wasn't right. They saw how the family treated me. They
heard The Old Lady's cutting words to me all the while calling me

"Granddaughter," but they stayed silent. Only their eyes spoke to me: "I know something is wrong here, but it is not my place to say; I cannot get involved in this." So my life dragged on, slowly forward, like that of a beast of burden under the power of the whip.

Gradually, I was allowed to do other jobs, such as helping to set up merchandise in the displays. I was around more people when I did this but always under the suspicious eye of The Old Lady or her daughter. I was happy that I could be out front, hearing and seeing other people. It kept my mind off sad thoughts and held back my captors' cruelest words. It was while I was doing this new task that I met Judy. Though most of the renters were of Asian or Middle Eastern decent, Judy was not. She stood out in the way she dressed and in how she spoke—with a kindness that was both compassionate and strong. Her short brown hair was styled purposefully at her shoulders, and her eyes saw me in a way the others did not.

Unexpected Friendship
I noticed Judy from the first moment she walked in the door. There was something about this woman that was electric. Her style was elegant yet understated enough to make her approachable. Her hair was beautiful, her make-up flawless. Her face always had the hint of a smile. Not a person could walk by unnoticed by her. "Hello, how are you today?" she'd call out, even if she were already in the middle of another conversation at that moment. "Treating the Missus right, I hope," she'd say to a potential customer in a friendly way. "I have the perfect gift that says, 'I love you,'" she'd coax. It was hard not to notice Judy, or to feel like she was your best friend. I felt that way as

well, and even though the watchful eyes of The Old Lady and her daughter were upon me, I would sneak in a smile or wave to her when I could. Judy, being the friendly woman she was, would do the same. There were times I was drawn to talk to her, but I would change my path at the last minute out of fear of punishment from my captors. Something had begun to change in me. The day Judy came into my life, it was as if a light and rays of hope slowly began to pierce the darkness I felt each day.

Judy's Past

Judy had lived several lives of her own by this time. She had grown up in a wealthy community, but as impressive as that was, she had not had an ideal life. Her mother had divorced and remarried. Her stepfather had his favorites out of his three children. She, being his only stepchild, was not one of them. He owned several restaurants in the push area surrounding this wealthy community, yet Judy never ate there for free. Maybe it was then that she first had the idea to make enough money so that she would never feel second-hand again. She did manage to marry well on her second time around, and she worked side by side with Darrin, so they could afford the finer things in life, including a mansion-sized home not far from a well-known wealthy hot spot near the beach. But there are things that money can't buy.

Judy's husband, Darrin, had been sick for a long time. His heart and lungs had slowed the energetic and active man he had once been. Judy ran the business more and more by herself these days, as he became too sick to do it. It was during this time while

126

she was transitioning from a full-time business to a more part-time one that Judy came into my life. To downsize, she had rented out a small area in the building The Old Lady's Daughter owned and set up shop. Darrin was too ill on many days to even get out of the car, so Judy carried everything in alone, encouraged customers to buy, and packed things up at the end of the day. She did this five to seven days a week.

The whole downstairs of the shop was filled with vendors who paid rent to use a small section and sell their goods. Judy had rented such a space and was selling her own products to those who wandered through this flea market of sorts. She filled her tables with beautiful things. I often stole a glance as I walked past her section. She had noticed me, too, but unlike the others, she decided to cross the gulf between us. "Hi. What is your name?" she asked me one day. I could not speak very much English at the time and understanding it was extremely difficult. I knew I would be in trouble if the family saw me talking to anyone in a personal way, so I gave a brief nod and said, "Sharon." I kept my head down, attentively working. I had no idea at the time how important that first conversation would be. I don't think anyone did.

The Gifts

Business did not go as well as Judy hoped, but that didn't stop her from being generous. The woman loved to shop, but she loved getting deals all the more. It wasn't unusual for her, when buying her expensive Lancôme make-up products, to walk away with a second set for free. One of these times, she handed that free selection to

The Old Lady's Daughter. "I have noticed your ... is she your grand-daughter? ... that helps you each day. She has beautiful skin, but I wonder if she might like some make-up to bring out those gorgeous eyes of hers. I don't want to seem forward, but will you give this to her as a gift, from me?" That hint of a smile grew wide as Judy handed the expensive gift to her. Of course, The Daughter took it and thanked her for the kindness, for who wouldn't? Only months later did I learn that this wasn't the only gift Judy had given to me via The Daughter that never made it into my hands. Not one gift would I ever see. Still, Judy had no clue what was happening behind the scenes.

I could say a few words in English, but any communication in anything other than Chinese was very difficult, especially with customers. Yet, The Daughter still insisted I help out selling items and dealing with prospective buyers. She knew I had trouble with this. When I stumbled over a word or simply nodded, she was NOT happy and would scold me and say, "You are so stupid! Are you deaf?! What is wrong with you that you cannot speak even a few words?! Who could want you? Ayye, stupid girl!" I was always cut to the heart with such words. I wanted to do well. Was I really so stupid? Tears would fill my eyes. Why couldn't they be happy with me? I never realized that a few people who saw how they treated me would share it with Judy.

Friendly Curiosity

What one person views as a curse can be a tremendous blessing to another. "Ahh, that Judy! Who does she think she is? She talks so much, that's why she sells so little!" The Daughter said one day. Of course I heard what she said. When I wasn't bringing in goods from the back room, sweeping and cleaning, I was sitting with The Old Lady, softly patting her hand or back as she sat in a chair from which she could watch all the people, coming and going. When she grew tired, I would take her to the back to watch TV. As I listened to The Daughter complain, I thought, *How lucky for me that Judy loves to talk to everyone. She talks to me, too.* I must've smiled as I thought this, for The Daughter suddenly snapped, "What are you smiling about?" I said nothing. But I continued to smile, patting The Old Lady's arm, thinking about my new friend.

Judy's friendliness opened doors for her as well. She began conversations with so many people working around me that she began to hear the truth about my situation. At first, she was completely shocked and couldn't believe that I was not free to go wherever I wanted. For the first time, she began to watch The Old Lady, her daughter, and me carefully. She was told The Daughter often shouted at me and called me names, but because she didn't understand Mandarin, she had no idea. She watched my behavior around The Old Lady. *No, this couldn't be right ... Sharon is just being sweet and caring for her grandmother,* she thought. But The Old Lady never smiled at me; never gave me a hug or kiss; never spoke my name. Judy began to notice how The Old Lady's Daughter treated me, too. She always gave short, sharp commands. I was constantly given the hardest tasks and never given a break. I never laughed or smiled. Something wasn't right. How long could this talkative lady keep her mouth shut?

My Name is Also Freedom

I am sure there were others who thought that things were not quite right with the relationship I had with The Old Lady and her daughter. They treated me harshly and scolded me so often that if I had been simply an employee, I would've quit. But day after day I was there, hustling to work hard while they barked commands at me. *No, something was just not right,* Judy thought. It was this suspicion that led Judy to start asking the others that worked in the flea mart deeper questions.

Another lady, Marie, had noticed the strange behaviors as well. "I cannot get involved because the family knows me too well, but I want to give you some money for the young girl (meaning me) to help her in some way," Marie told Judy one day. I had no idea any of this was going on. So many times I longed for someone to help, to notice, to at least acknowledge my plight, but no one ever did. I had pretty much given up that idea.

Building Trust

Judy and I continued our friendship secretly. I would walk past her booth slowly, and we'd exchange smiles or a word or two. This went on for nearly a year before I felt I could truly trust her.

"Sharon, this is not right. They don't treat you like a human being. It's so wrong," Judy said to me one day after she'd learned about my situation. "Why don't you call the police?" "I'm scared. Where I go?" I said. "Where I gonna go?" I was fearful of what would happen to me. I thought I would just be brought back to them and things would become unbearable. I was so fearful. This was my family. What could I do? "I will help you," she said. At that moment I knew I could trust her.

The Wrong Meat

I have mentioned how I hated shopping with The Daughter, but if she wanted me to go, I had to. There were a very few times she couldn't go with me, and she sent me with the grandson's girlfriend or someone else. She would tell me what to get and give me a list. How on earth could I read this list? I did my best to memorize all of the items on it. I pushed the cart around the store and collected everything. There was one thing, a cut of beef, that I was not familiar with. I stopped for quite a while at the meat section, trying desperately to read the labels. I finally had to take a guess and picked up a large packet of meat and put it in the cart.

"What?! What is this?!" The Daughter shouted when we returned. "I cannot use this for our supper. It is not the right meat! What is wrong with you, you stupid girl! I gave you a list and told you everything I needed!" She began to scream and curse and eventually her mother, The Old Lady, got involved. "I told you she was worthless! And this piece of meat is more expensive," she said, looking at the receipt. "I see what you are trying to do, you thief!" Since we had been in America, some of the more violent attacks from The Old Lady had lessened when others were in the house, so it took me completely by surprise when she suddenly kicked me and then reached out and grabbed my hair, like she had done in Taiwan. She started to drag me like she had done before, but she was too old, and I was much stronger. I yelled so loud she let go, thinking her daughter's husband might hear. I ran down the hall to the bathroom and locked myself in. I was breathing heavy and crying hard. My neck hurt, and I was already having trouble with my back constantly aching. I was concerned that she had already done permanent damage. Something broke in me. I knew something had to change. "This is it!" I said to myself. "I can't do this ... I can't anymore ... I just can't ... "

The Phone Number

The next day, sore, I returned with The Old Lady and her daughter to the shop. Judy had been renting her spot in the shop for nearly a year, but with Darrin being sick and her becoming older, she knew that her time working like this was at its end. She thought about me a lot and realized that others around me might not be as bold as she had been towards me, and she felt she couldn't so easily abandon me without leaving some thread for me to hang on to. She decided to give me her phone number before she left. She found the back of a receipt and tore a small corner from it. Purposely writing each number as clearly as possible, she folded the small strip of paper and hid it in her hand. She made her rounds, as she usually did, greeting the others, chatting a bit here and there in the harmlessly flirty way she had. I saw her move closer and closer to where I was working. She always had a smile and a cheery comment for me, sometimes she winked or even blew a few kisses in my direction. I loved this woman. I felt human around her. This time, as she came to greet me, she reached out her hand, carefully grabbing my own in hers. I felt something in her palm. It wrinkled slightly, and I grasped it subconsciously. I dared not look at what was now balled up in my hand. "If you need *anything*—call me. Be careful," she whispered, acting as if she had asked me something else so no one would know. "Goodbye." I nodded and smiled and pulled back my hand with the small, wadded-up piece of paper in it and placed it in my pocket.

The Plan

The horror of the previous night stayed with me, and I had decided what I needed to do. Now I had a connection and a phone number to help me out of this prison.

There were no windows in the storeroom in the back of the shop, and everyone pretty much ignored it. Because the bathroom was there, I had a good reason to be back there from time to time without fear of getting in trouble. I knew I could use the phone in there without anyone knowing. I could never use the phone at home. There, they watched me like a hawk.

My opportunity came one Thursday. The Old Lady and her daughter had made an appointment to get their hair done together. The family had a girl who kept an eye on me from time to time, and there were also cameras everywhere. I had a short window of time that I could go to the workshop and use the phone to call Judy to let her know what time I planned to leave. Tonight was the night. I felt I had just one chance, and this was it.

I walked to the workshop, opened the door and slowly walked in. I picked up the phone. My heart beat so loudly I thought it would jump right out of my chest! I took a deep breath, unfolded my precious scrap of paper, and dialed the numbers. "Hello. Judy?" I said cautiously. "This Sharon; I ok, need help to leave." I continued to try to tell of my plan in broken English. I only hoped she understood what I needed and was still willing to help.

"You must call the police," Judy instructed me after I had told her my plan to escape. "I am not sure what to do ... " Her voice trailed off, and I heard her talking to her husband. I heard some muffled words, but then Judy's voice returned to the phone, strong and clear. "Ok. I can come pick you up. Tell me when and where."

This was it. This was REALLY it. I had never thought about running away before. Where would I go? Now I had some place, even if it was for a short time, I would at least be away from this family and their hate and abuse. Determination filled me as my hand shook, the phone still held to my ear. I spoke with confidence as I told Judy the address, making sure she understood. I repeated it again. Then I finished by saying, "7:30 p.m. Thursday night. Come that time. I outside. I ready."

Part IV
Finding Freedom

Chapter 12

The Escape

My heart was pounding so loud I could feel the blood pulsing in my ears. Every nerve in my body was on alert. Did I hear someone behind me? My toes were wet and cold and bits of green grass stuck between them. I hardly noticed the water that puddled at my feet. I mechanically moved the end of the hose back and forth. "Keep watering the grass and flowers. No one must suspect a thing," I nervously commanded myself. The slow rushing of the water from the hose and the nightly sounds on the block were forced into the distant background as my eyes nervously darted up and down the street, searching for the car that belonged to my savior, Judy, who I knew would soon be here.

I had rolled the garbage cans to the curb and began to water the grass, like I did every Thursday night, the only task I did unattended, a brief moment away from the watchful eyes of my captors. It was a typical warm August night in 2005. I wore the same dirty green shorts, paper thin from being worn day after day and a dingy white blouse dotted with brown flowers that hung oddly over my boney frame. I had taken off my sandals to keep them from getting wet as I stood now, in the middle of the front lawn, trying hard not to shake from the exhilarating fear and anticipation that gripped my entire body.

I took a deep breath. The puddle at my feet grew larger and a small, snakelike stream of water slowly crept forward, reaching the sidewalk. How long could I stand out here without being called back into that house, that suffocating prison of mine? A car rolled slowly down the street. Could it be? It continued past me only to pull into a driveway at the far end of the block. Thump, thump, thump, the blood continued to pulse, this time I felt it on the sides of my head, keeping time—as the slow, painful seconds dragged on and on. I absent-mindedly wiggled my toes as the water poured over them. Tonight *had* to be the night. It had to! My thoughts trailed back to the night before when I had helped The Old Lady take her bath and then massaged her feet until she fell asleep. I had soothed her late into the night, as I usually did, until deep sleep fell over her, and it was well past midnight.

Goodbye, Grandma

The Old Lady lay there asleep. I looked at her face—how old she had become, yet still her skin was soft and youthful. I continued to pat her hand. It was so automatic now; I did it without thinking. I knew what I had to do next. I took a deep breath and bent closer to her and quietly said, "Grandma, I wish you had treated me right, like a real granddaughter. You told everyone I was your granddaughter, but I am not. I just wanted to be treated like a person, a human being. I wish I could go back in time and change things, but I cannot. I would never leave you in this way, by running away. I would have appreciated you for the rest of my life if you had only shown me some respect, but you did not; you treated me shamefully as a slave. I cannot serve you or help you anymore."

I whispered all this to her, her heavy breathing drowning out most of my words. "Why wouldn't you accept me? Why couldn't you love me? I tried so hard to please you and love you in return. Why couldn't I be good enough for you? But I must go. I have to go." My confession had ended with, "I'm sorry ... " I was surprised to feel a small tear roll to the edge of my nose and slowly fall onto my knee. Physically and emotionally drained, I lay down on the floor near the Old Lady's bed and covered myself with a single, tattered, dirty blanket. Cupping my hands together for a pillow, I fell asleep. When I awoke the next day, I knew it would be my last with this 'family' of mine.

Suddenly, I was snapped back into the moment as I noticed a long dark sedan cruise by the house. Wait. I had seen this same car before; this was the second time it had circled past me. It continued down the street and turned to make its third pass, hoping the street was clear and that I had seen it. It was her. I knew it had to be her! The pounding of my heart grew so loud I could no longer distinguish it from the other sounds around me. My body felt heavy and tense. I thought I might jump right out of my skin if I had to wait a second longer. The car I had eyed rolled to a stop at the end of the street, its brake lights giving me a gentle wink: "You know it's time; I am here to take you away from all this." For a moment, I was frozen. I told my feet to run, but nothing happened. The opportunity to leave this horrid life was shouting at me, and incredibly, I was too paralyzed to take it. What was I waiting for?

Then, as if a gunshot had gone off, signifying the beginning of a great race, I bolted. I dropped the hose, running as fast as I could towards the end of the street and that dark, silent sedan patiently waiting for me. Everything I owned I left behind, except my tattered shirt and pants that didn't quite fit right, the clothes reminding me of the life I had been living these past twenty years, a torn and ravaged life. In my bare, wet feet I ran in fear. I was sure that someone was chasing me, that an arm would reach out to grab me. I did not dare look back. Would I reach the car in time? I felt the warm, rough pavement tearing at the bottoms of my feet, threatening to slow me down. How far that distance to the end of the block seemed to be to me! It went on forever. I reached the handle on the back door and jerked it open. I jumped into the back seat of the car, pulling the door shut behind me. Without a sound, we sped on as if nothing had happened. Gasping for air, my heart still pounding, my ears pulsing, I felt lightheaded. I fearfully looked back through the small, tinted window. I saw no one. It was quiet and still and dark. I continued to look back in disbelief. The summer sky had made this night glow, a deep royal blue, perfect, beautiful. Did I really just do this? My breathing was heavy, and my hands shook uncontrollably. I felt a slight sickening feeling in my stomach, as I hoped this was not all some dream. When I could no longer see the house or even a glimpse of the street where I had lived in bondage, I finally turned away to see where I was headed. For my sleeping captors and the upscale neighborhood they lived in, it was just another Thursday night.

Although Judy and her husband, Darrin—not yet realizing the true scope of this rescue—were calm, my head was still spinning from my grand escape. "Dink, dink, dink, dink," the sedan signaled as we drove up the ramp onto the freeway. After some time, we made our way closer to their quiet, secluded house near the beach. "You must be hungry. Let's stop and pick up something. How about some burgers?" Judy suggested. I had eaten a hamburger only once before. Several of The Old Lady's grandchildren had picked some up and, in a forgetful moment, offered me one. It had been a wonderful treat from the usual soured leftovers. The car heaved and bumped as we pulled up into the parking lot. The neon yellow and red sign of the restaurant was oddly comforting. Even though I continued to insist that I wasn't a bit hungry, I managed to eat the entire burger, fries and extra-large shake we got before we eventually made it to her front door.

My New Home

Judy's house was beautiful! She led me upstairs and told me to relax and get cleaned up. I had forgotten that I was still barefoot and small blades of grass and bits of dirt clung to my feet, legs, and ankles. "If you'd like, you can take a shower. Use whatever soaps

and shampoos you find," Judy said. Her soothing voice offered me
such peace and comfort. Use whatever soaps and shampoos I could
find? I was never allowed to use anything but dish soap on myself,
and a shower with clean running water was out of the question. I
took a long, hot shower. There was scented soap, floral shampoo ...
I rubbed it over every inch of me. It felt good. I let the wonderful,
pure water pour over me for a long time. I hadn't felt this clean in
such a very long time. I stepped out of the shower and dried myself
with a large, soft towel that lay folded on the counter, placed there
for me. The energy and adrenaline that had gotten me to this place
began to fade, and suddenly I felt very tired. It was late, and my
body was telling me that I had run a marathon that day. I had been
running a lot longer than that most of my life. I wanted to relax, just
sleep, but my mind was still geared up, and the fear and anxiety of
being found out and sent back to that place—to those people—kept
nagging at me.

A Bed of My Own

I think Judy could see that I was exhausted, and a good night's sleep
would be best for all of us, so she led me upstairs into her guest
bedroom. A room to myself was incredible enough, but a bed to
sleep in, and all to myself? I felt like I had gone to Heaven. Clean
blankets and pillows and a comforter covered in the most beautiful
flower pattern spilled over the bed. Its colors matched the walls
and carpet, and gorgeous smells filled the room! Judy hastily found
something I could sleep in. It was a far cry from what I was used
to. She apologized for its size and promised we would shop for

something proper the next day. In my broken English and tearful gratitude I thanked her over and over, but she would have none of it. "Nonsense!" she replied. "You go to sleep, and we'll do this clothes thing proper in the morning." As I lay there in the bed, I stretched out my arms. I felt soft, fluffy bed on either side, without end. I rolled to the right and then to the left. Still, the bed continued. I felt overwhelmed inside at the day's events. "God, I thank you so much for helping me, for bringing Judy to me to help me. Please, help me tomorrow to face what may come." Emotions and thoughts swirled around in my head for quite a while as I lay there waiting for sleep to come. It did, and it stayed. The sun came up, and I was still asleep. Something happened that I could never remember ever happening to me before: I stayed in bed until I wanted to get up.

Like a Princess

Judy was an amazing yet eccentric older woman. Her sense of style was incredible. She wasted no time in taking me to the mall for clothes shopping. Her specialty: shoes! My whole body tingled with excitement and delight as we pulled up to one of the biggest malls in the state. I had never seen such a place! Shop after shop of clothes, shoes, purses, and accessories filled my eyes. Then we walked into Nordstrom. Oh my! I had never seen such beautiful things. "First thing is to get some shoes for you," Judy said in such a serious tone. It was as if she was on a mission to erase every part of that downtrodden slave that I had been. "What size do you wear?" She casually tossed her words my way, but they hit me like a bowling ball. What size *did* I wear? I had no idea. I felt my face begin to burn as embarrassment slowly filled my cheeks. All of my clothes and shoes had been given to me by others and never fit me quite right. I wore them until they were either too tight to put on or they were falling apart from daily wear. What size did I wear? A lump formed in my throat as I meekly said, "I not know ... I never buy shoe ... " My voice trailed off, hoping Judy would understand. Like a machine, she continued to scan the merchandise, not fazed a bit by my reply. "Oh yes, these ones, try these on." She handed me the first pair of brand-new shoes I had ever held in my hands. They were light silver in color with a thin strap across the back, allowing the back of the heel to show. The straps wove around in a herringbone pattern to the front of the shoe and then tied in a neat bow with the ends slightly dangling down the sides, highlighting the toe of the shoe, which looked like a ballerina's slipper. I fell in love with these shoes! As I slipped my bare, calloused feet inside, I felt like Cinderella, no longer among the ashes. Hope that a princess was inside of me became all too possible. Although the shoes were flats, I walked around in them rather awkwardly, never having walked in any type of heel before. I had no time to get use to them, however, because we were on to the next purchase and the next. There was no other way to describe it: It was a feast of shopping!

I believe that Judy was just as excited to shop for me as I was to receive her wonderful gifts. She spared no expense on herself and she extended that to me. I had somehow stumbled across a savior of sorts in this wonderful woman, and I would forever be grateful to her and the kindness she poured upon me.

The Escape

I was so caught up in my first day of freedom that I never thought about what might be happening back at the house with The Old Lady and her daughter. My loyalty and total surrender to their daily demands had kept them from ever thinking that I might have run away or escaped. They were sure I had been kidnapped or had somehow become lost. With no sign of me in the house that night, they called the police and made a full report.

Sharon Is Missing

"I was upstairs, taking a nap, I guess, when I awoke suddenly and called for Sharon," The Daughter told the police officers who had just arrived at the house in response to the call about a missing person. "I hurried downstairs and began to search the house. I looked everywhere, calling her name, but when I couldn't find her, I called my husband to see if he had seen Sharon."

"I had been working on some paperwork for my business when I heard Sharon outside, dragging the trash cans around to the backyard. She is so small, you know, she has a hard time managing them," he went on. "I tell her to leave them, it's ok, I can handle them," he continued, adding a few lies to his story. When had anyone ever offered me help? There were much harder chores than this that I did completely on my own, even when I was sick. I got no help then. "I don't remember hearing her come back in. It wasn't until my wife asked me where Sharon was that I remembered hearing her outside," he explained. "It was around—" His wife cut in then, "Sharon waters the lawn and brings the trash cans in from

145

the street every Thursday. She always comes in after that. It's just not like her. I don't understand. I went outside and saw the hose laying on the ground, water still gushing from the end, and a pair of shoes left on the lawn. I became worried and sent my husband to search for her." Her husband cleared his throat and began again, "I decided to walk through the neighborhood and down towards the school, thinking she may have gotten lost. I asked everyone I saw if they had seen her, but no one had. I walked slowly through the park but saw nothing. It was as if she vanished into thin air." The police continued to ask question after question, hoping to find a clue. "Did she go out or perhaps drive somewhere?" "She doesn't drive or go anywhere alone," was the reply. "What about her friends? Maybe she is with them," the officers inquired further. "She has no—not many friends," was the answer.

Every question led to a dead end. Sharon goes nowhere. Sharon has no friends. Sharon doesn't drive. The picture they painted of me was an odd one. Maybe I was a mentally or emotionally stunted young woman in their eyes. I don't think the thought occurred to them that I was a slave living in this wealthy community and had finally seen a window of opportunity to escape my personal hell.

The officers began canvassing the neighborhood, interviewing everyone. They even interviewed the family pastor. Interview after interview revealed nothing. Sharon was missing, and those around her seemed to know nothing about her at all.

The Escape

On the News

The unusual news that a small Asian woman, perhaps mentally impaired, was wandering lost or possibly abducted in a rather well-off town, became the headline of the local news. Suddenly a picture of me was all over the television. It didn't occur to me that people may have seen both me and Judy shopping and that it looked suspicious. A woman who had seen that report on the news began to follow us from store to store. As we carried our treasures to the car, the woman wrote down our license plate number and contacted the police.

"On August 18, 2005 at approximately 9 p.m., local resident Sharon [Ho] was reported missing from her residential area. Anyone with information regarding this matter is asked to call the local police department."
—Official Police Report, August, 2005

I hadn't a clue local news had shown a photo of me as a missing person and that a search was underway. Judy's husband, after seeing the report himself and worrying that he could be getting mixed up in something he might not have all the facts about, had also called the police himself. When I arrived back at Judy's house and began unpacking all my brand-new clothes, two officers knocked at the door, asking about me and hoping to get to the bottom of things. This would soon lead to a house full of enforcement agents, all trying to piece together what could be an international incident.

My Name is Also Freedom

"Based on a tip received from a citizen who recognized Ms. [Ho] from television media coverage, police detectives, assisted by members of the Sheriff's Department, have located Ms. [Ho] on the evening of August 19, 2005."
—Official Police Report, August, 2005

"Can we please speak to Ms. Ho?" the uniformed men asked as Darrin answered the door. "The police are here?" Judy said, as she heard the discussion from upstairs. I was so scared, I didn't know what to do. She joined her husband and the officers at the door, but I panicked. I couldn't go back to The Old Lady. I was so overcome by such a powerful fear that I hid in one of the closets. When the officers and Judy and Darrin came looking for me, I was so frightened I refused to come out. After a time of pleading, promising me that everything would be alright, I finally came out and threw myself at the feet of a young officer.

Please ... No Send Me Back!

I fell to my knees, clinging to his ankles, begging him not to send me back to such a horrible place. Tears streamed down my face as I managed to choke out in broken English, pleading, "Please, no send me back, please! I no go back—it be bad for me to go back, please, no—" I broke down in a puddle on the floor, sobbing, grasping his pant legs. I don't think he knew what to do. Stunned, I heard him mutter under his breath, "What the—?" I think he was just as overcome as I was because slowly he knelt down next to me, his face filled with compassion, and promised me he wouldn't send me any-

The Escape

where I didn't want to go. "It's gonna be okay," he calmly repeated over and over to me. "I am not taking you anywhere." In moments, the house filled with more officers of all kinds, and I overheard a radio call to have a translator sent in to help. I was led to the table in the kitchen where I sat down and began my best to tell my story. They told me The Family was looking for me, and they had reported me as a missing person. Judy set a hot cup of tea in front of me and began taking coffee orders from all who wanted some. The translator arrived as well, a tall, handsome young man, who had the kindest eyes. He began trying several languages, Cantonese, Mandarin, until I replied, "Yes, I understand." I wiped my face on a napkin, and a warm feeling of safety fell over me.

It took quite some time to unravel the details of what had happened, why I had left The Old Lady and her daughter. The officers wrote down every detail as the investigation went very late into the night.

" ... So far, our investigation has revealed that [said person] left her home of her own free will and accord and is in good health. Police detectives are continuing to investigate this matter. Based on the continuing investigation and upon the wishes of Ms. [Ho], no further information relating to the reason for her leaving, her current location, or any other information will be released at this time.
The important information is that Ms. [Ho] left her residence of her own volition and that she has been located and is safe."
—Official Police Report, August, 2005

149

The Search Warrant

The information that I gave to the police officers that night set off all kinds of red flags about why I had left and what was going on back at The Daughter's house. There was plenty of suspicion that I was a victim of human trafficking and that my 'family' was somehow involved. The case was referred to the Human Trafficking Division of Homeland Security Investigations. A search warrant was needed so evidence could be collected. This assignment had reached a young Homeland Security Special Agent who had to write an affidavit in support of a search warrant and then get it signed by a federal judge quickly. It was Sunday, and the agent learned that the judge was at a local amusement park with his family on his day off. "What?!" the agent said as he put the papers in a folder and headed to his car. "I gotta find this judge by checking every ride and show in the park? Well, I wish I had time for a rollercoaster ride or two myself." As he clipped the seatbelt around his waist and started the engine, his partner jumped in and shut the door. "Never a dull moment, huh?" he commented, as they pulled out and onto the street. This agent would become such a blessing to me; always fighting for me. He would make sure he kept in touch with me through the years, always hoping things would work out for me and that life would be better.

A team of Homeland Security special agents, all wearing tactical gear, showed up at the house of The Daughter, her husband, and The Old Lady. They presented a warrant to them to read. I am sure they were all pretty scared, not knowing what was happening.

The Escape

The agents split up and began to search every inch of the house. One by one, the officers questioned everyone in the house separately. Both The Daughter and her husband refused to say a word, but not The Old Lady. As she answered each question, more and more details came to light about what my life was like and how I came to live with her. I had never been separated from The Old Lady in all the years I had lived with her. If there was anyone who knew all the answers, it was her. In her truthfulness, she never realized she had provided key information to the agents that would later help me a great deal. The house was searched, computers seized, and interviews conducted, including of several neighbors. All of this was just the beginning of my struggle to stay free, which would take many twists and turns and force the secrets this family held about me out into the open. I would have many lawyers, police officers and federal agents, case workers, and countless others taking up my cause, and it would take a few years, eventually even thrusting me back to face that family. But for now, I was free and just beginning to understand the challenges of living free.

Go to freedomhasaname.com/shari for tips on how to recognize human trafficking.

Chapter 13

My Name is Shari Ho

If there was one good thing that I learned from all those years of serving The Old Lady, it was an appreciation for well-made clothes, clothes that had a lot of style and fashion. Day after day, since I was barely big enough to reach the hangers, I had laid out her beautifully tailor-made clothes, her colorful silks and furs, hand-stitched by the finest Chinese clothing makers. I had a natural gift, I guess, at putting colors and styles together, and I enjoyed doing it. But now, living with Judy, a well-off stylish woman herself, I was bound to go shopping at some point, and shopping we went!

You may have heard of stories of people who were lost in the desert, starving, and near dying of thirst. When they are finally rescued, they have to be very careful not to allow themselves to gorge on food and water too soon, for it could be very damaging to their health. Though the lack of money held me back somewhat, I was that person, starved inside, but now I was in heaven as we hit store after store, and I enjoyed every minute of it! It was strange for me to think that just weeks before, I had been waiting on that family every minute in my tattered old clothes, hoping for enough to eat, and now I was treated like a princess. "What do you need? What would you like for breakfast? What shop should we go to next?" Judy would ask. It was so unreal to me.

My New Routine

Every morning, Judy let me sleep late. *Every day* until after 10 a.m.! I'd hear her say to her husband, "Let her sleep. She needs her rest." She cooked breakfast for me and washed my clothes every day. She became like a mother to me. I will never forget this—being truly treated like a daughter. I was loved by her. I even started calling her Mom.

Sharon No Longer

It was Judy who suggested I change my name. "You told me that The Old Lady gave you the name Sharon? Judy asked me one day. "Well, you are not her slave anymore, why keep that name?" I thought this was a pretty good idea, so I responded with, "What name, Mom, you want?" Putting her hand on her chin, she looked at me with a sparkle in her eye and said, "I like the name Shari. What do you think?" "Yes, Mom, I now Shari." I gave her a hug, and we both laughed together.

The HTTF

The Human Trafficking Task Force (HTTF) is an incredible organization.

It is a collaboration of law enforcement, victim service providers, non-profit organizations, faith-based organizations, government entities, and the community. Its mission is to work together, taking a victim-centered approach, with the common goal of combating human trafficking and related crimes.

Among the organizations that make up the HTTF are local Police Departments and Community Service Programs, the Highway Patrol, the District Attorney's Office, the local Sheriff's Department, The Salvation Army, the Department of Homeland Security, and various non-profit organizations. Collaboratively, with over 60 organizations to close gaps in services, they assist victims of human trafficking.

Since 2004, the HTTF has assisted over 500 victims of human trafficking from thirty-six countries, with the majority from the United States. The HTTF had only been operating for a little more than a year when I escaped The Old Lady in 2005.

It was the HTTF that brought Amy Henry into my life.

My First Case Manager

Three days after I had escaped from The Old Lady and her daughter, I was connected with the HTTF. When the police had come to Judy's house that night, Community Services Program, Victim Assistance Program, had contacted Amy Henry and arranged for me to meet with her. Human trafficking victims receive a case manager to deal with any immediate needs—work visas, green cards, housing—so survivors, such as myself, could transition into a more "normal" way of life. Amy Henry was my first case manager. Amy had been working with The Cambodian Family with the Partnership for Trafficking Victim Services, working specifically with foreign national victims of trafficking and was an HTTF founding member. I was so scared and nervous at the time. I only felt safe at Judy's house and wasn't sure what was going to happen next.

"Shari," Judy called to me from downstairs. "I want to talk to you about something." Her voice trailed off as I made my way down the stairs into the kitchen. "The Victim Witness Program has case workers who are assigned to people who have gone through what you have gone through. Why don't we see how they can help? We have an appointment to meet with case manager Amy Henry tomorrow. I'll be there with you. We'll eat lunch and just talk about how you can get help to live so you won't ever have to worry about The Old Lady or her daughter again."

I trusted Judy. She had been the only one to see what was going on in my life and had cared enough to reach out to me. I was free because of her. "Okay, I go," I replied, still feeling a bit nervous. The next day we drove to the restaurant where we were to meet Amy. "I thought meeting here might be a little less stressful than in some stuffy office," Judy explained as the waitress led us to a spacious table near the back. "Thank you. We are expecting a friend to join us," Judy told her. The waitress passed out menus and took our drink orders. This was a strange world to me. I was not allowed to eat out with The Old Lady and her daughter. If I wasn't cooking for them at home, they usually had me pick up food they had ordered, but here I was, sitting in a restaurant like everyone else, given a menu and being waited on for the first time. My nerves gave way to the joy I felt at being treated like a normal human being.

Amy Henry

"Hi. I'm Amy Henry," a voice suddenly spoke from behind me. "You must be Judy? And are you Shari?" We all shook hands, and she sat down across from me. "I heard about your story and want to tell you how brave I think you are to have escaped the way you did. You don't have to worry. You will NEVER have to go back with that family," she assured me. "I want you to know that I am here to help you and get you all the assistance you need—any paperwork, money, a place to stay—anything that you might need. I know you don't really know me right now, but I hope you come to trust me. I am here to help you. I really am." Amy went on to encourage me and reassure me that everything was going to be okay. Our meeting was not a very long one, but Amy asked if she could come by Judy's house in a day or two to talk more. I felt good inside. I was still unsure about all that was happening around me, but something inside said it was all going to be okay. I guess I believed Amy at that moment. This was the good day I had been looking for in all my bad days. After all those nights I had spent telling myself that tomorrow would be better, maybe, finally, better days had come.

Since 2003, Amy had worked with foreign-born women (and men) who had been freed from sexual exploitation and forced labor and were rebuilding their lives. As part of the HTTF, Amy

157

worked with other professionals to identify and care for victims of trafficking and to build a network of social service providers who were willing to care for victims and prevent trafficking from happening in their own community. Amy also spoke regularly about human trafficking. Amy loved working with the faith-based community groups and later introduced me to The Salvation Army. This was Amy's passion, which has led her to travel to over twenty-eight countries.

Amy kept her promise and came to visit me a day or two later. We talked about a lot of things during that second meeting. I led her upstairs to show her my room. "This where I hide. Police come to house, but I so scared," I said, opening the closet door. I began to feel more comfortable with this case manager. Soon, I was showing her my new shoes, the ones Judy had bought me that first night I had run away. I was so excited. I just talked and talked! Amy thought my shoes were so cute. "I love the color! They look like the shoes of a princess," she said. This was the beginning of one of the most important relationships I would have in my life. I would rely on this new friend for over a year and a half, and she would eventually add one more country to that list of those she has visited—my native Taiwan.

Many Things to Learn

"Do you know how to count?" Amy asked me one day. Part of Amy's job was to teach me the skills I needed to be independent. I thought about her question and remembered my mom asking that same thing, "Count ten days. I will come back for you," she'd said.

Then I said to Amy, "Yeah. When I little, ah, yeah," I kept that old thought to myself. I knew I needed to count more numbers than up to ten. "I learn," I responded.

"Okay, we are going to learn how to shop and use money, so let's start with twenty dollars," Amy explained. "Have you been grocery shopping before?" I had been many times with The Old Lady and The Daughter, but I never paid for anything or picked out things other than what they told me to pick. "Let's say we take a walk to the store and buy some things?" Amy suggested. When we reached the market, we went inside and looked around a bit. "What kinds of things do you like to eat? We can start with some basics," Amy instructed. "Let's get a cart, look at the prices, and see what we can get with twenty dollars." At first, Amy just walked with me, letting me look and pick things out, but I found this very hard to do. After quite a while, I had only picked two things and was becoming frustrated. "Wow, maybe I set the goal a little too high for today," Amy said, a bit shocked at my struggle. "I'll help this time." So we went to the produce section and picked out some vegetables and fruit and then moved on to bread. We talked about the prices as Amy pointed out the signs. Things sold by the pound were weighed on a scale; other items were priced as marked. It was a lot to remember, but Amy reminded me this was only our first trip. Then we stood in line, and she showed me how to pay for it. I was grateful Amy didn't embarrass me. I was an adult and very conscious of the fact I didn't know things that even little kids already knew.

More Lessons

"I brought the ads with me today, "Amy said as she walked in the door one day. "We're gonna practice looking at the store ads, finding things you want to buy, adding them up, and then subtracting them from ten dollars, okay?" she explained as she opened the paper and smoothed it out on the table. We spent hours doing this. It was kind of fun and less stressful than facing a person in the market. I got pretty good at what things I might want and knowing how to make change for a ten-dollar bill.

Becoming More Independent

I remember my first time at Mother's Market after I had escaped. I ordered the same things The Daughter had always ordered for her and her mother—bread, a sandwich, spinach, tofu, fish, cheese, and a pickle—and I ate it all myself! It felt so good! I think it cost twelve dollars. I gave them twenty dollars and got eight dollars back!

At first, when I went to stores and places to buy things it was always with Amy or Judy. Later, I went by myself. In all those times I can't remember anyone ever cheating me out of change. Many times I didn't know how to add prices properly. The first time I went all by myself, I got so frustrated and embarrassed that I walked out. I cried when I got outside the door. Usually people were always helpful when they saw that I struggled.

Money

Early on, my case manager would reimburse Judy for the cost of whatever supplies I needed. One of the first things I bought was

160

a phone. Amy came with me. "A phone is very important to have. You'll need it a lot," she said. There were contracts to sign, and I was glad she was there to help explain it all to me.

Judy loved to shop, and we enjoyed doing this together. We'd shop and laugh and have such fun. I was excited every time we'd go out. I *wanted* to buy things, especially shoes. I LOVE shoes! I didn't know what the styles were at that time, just whether I thought they looked good on me. I tried them all on. When it came to shoes and pants, I always had to try them on first. I was a size zero at that time! Pants were always too long, and I would go to the kids section in order to find something that would be the right length. I really like soft materials, but I never really liked jeans. I would have my clothes altered because it was cheaper back then. Clothes could be expensive, and when I was shopping with Judy, we went to Nordstrom and other high-end stores.

Ross

Then I found Ross. It was love at first sight! I remember when I felt confident enough to go to Ross all by myself. I always paid with a ten-dollar bill. I looked at the price and knew what six dollars or seven dollars was and what the change would be; I knew how to count to ten. Using a twenty-dollar bill was still hard for me. I knew one, two, three, four, but not really much more after that.

I bought a lot of clothes when I shopped. I guess I had to make up for all the ones I didn't have. As a slave, the colors I wore were mostly blue or pink or crazy bright like orange or red. I now

161

felt drawn to black and grey as colors. I don't know why. I loved black then, when I was first set free. I like colors now. My favorite color is green. I really didn't know how to budget in those days, so clothes were always first on my shopping list.

Mio

I walked just about everywhere I went, but in the U.S., people drive everywhere. If you don't have a license, then public transportation is a must. My next lesson was learning to ride the bus. I met so many wonderful people through the HTTF. One of those new friends was Mio, a young Japanese graduate student who helped me with life skills. Riding the bus was one of those skills.

Mio spent days mapping out a route, even wait times at the bus stop. Then she rode the route herself, to make sure everything would go smoothly. This was only a three-mile trip, but Mio wanted my first trip to be a success. "Okay, we'll ride it together and then you'll be ready for your first trip alone. Don't worry. I'll follow behind you in the car," she said with a smile. We stood at the bus stop, the bus pulled up, and I boarded. I dropped the coins in the slot and found a seat near a window as the bus pulled away. Mio pulled away, too, and followed the bus. She knew which way the bus was going. When it stopped, she stopped and waited for it to continue its route. The driver of the bus saw Mio in the rearview mirror, following closely. When he stopped, she stopped. This was beginning to concern him. The route he was supposed to take was a straight line, but he abruptly changed the route as he turned left, then right, trying to shake this car that had been following him.

Mio was confused at why the driver didn't follow his route, but she had no way to tell the driver what she was doing, so she just kept following. Suddenly the bus came to a halt and the driver jumped out and began yelling at Mio. She was able to explain to him what was happening. "My friend is on the bus. I just wanted to make sure she was okay." The bus driver laughed and said, "I was going to call the cops on you!" We both had a good laugh about that!

Mio didn't give up on me and continued to tutor me, even helping me to study to get a learner's permit to drive. She'd visit restaurants and write out whole menus for me to practice with, so when I went out I could order. She worked with me for four years. She was such a good friend!

My First Job

I was determined to work for myself and earn my own money. As grateful as I was for Judy's help and her kindness in letting me live with her, I knew that to really be free I had to provide for myself, and that meant getting a job. I had been living at Judy's for close to nine months now. It was sad to have to leave, but it was time to move on.

"Mom, it so hard, I leave. I so thankful for all you done. I miss you," I said as we tearfully hugged goodbye. But both of us knew this was the right thing to do. Judy had a friend who was willing to let me move in with her. Her name was Elsa. All of her children but her son had left home, and she had an extra room she said I could stay in. She had a large house and yard with a large dog. I had met this woman briefly when I was still living with The Old Lady and her daughter; she had walked into the shop with Judy while I was working one day. She seemed kind, and although at that time she hadn't known my story, she was now very sympathetic to my situation. She had a housekeeper of her own, but I often helped out with chores around the house, cooking for her son and walking the dog. I decided to live with Elsa, get a job, and save enough money to live on my own. Elsa lived within walking distance to many job opportunities, so this seemed like a good plan.

Amy and others at the HTTF had worked hard and fast to get the paperwork in motion for me to have the proper documents to work and to stay in the U.S. That is when I found a preschool very close to Elsa's house that offered me a job working with toddlers. I spoke little English, and my job skills were limited. I even needed help filling out the job application! But I knew I was a hard worker and a very fast learner. They hired me, paying me minimum wage. I would be paid every two weeks.

My First Paycheck

I was so excited to get that first paycheck. I had to ask Elsa, "How much this?"

"It's five hundred dollars," she said, which seemed like a fortune to me at the time. "I rich!" I excitedly told her. She shook her head and laughed. I decided to save as much of the money as I could because I didn't have to pay her rent at that time. She talked me into going to the bank to open an account.

My Name is Shari Ho

"What do you mean, she can't open a savings account?" Elsa said to the bank clerk in astonishment. "I'm very sorry, but you must have a second form of identification—just a work I.D. won't do," the teller said apologetically. "Well, we'll try someplace else, I guess," Elsa said. We went to several other banks in the area but had the same problem everywhere. Then we walked into Union Bank. They were wonderful! It was the only bank to accept me so I could cash my check. I was nervous every single time I went to the bank. I brought extra deposit slips home with me because I was so conscious of people staring at me at the bank. I needed help filling it out. I'd sometimes ask the people at the bank to help. Some did, some didn't. I practiced writing numbers over and over again. I am much better at it now. I can write up to 12,000, but I need help after that! I have my own little way of figuring things out.

Preschool

Working at the preschool was not very glamourous. I mostly changed diapers and cleaned classrooms—the dirtier jobs—and I did every one of them! I also had to cook, which I was very good at, and make snacks for the kids. I had to remember everything they told me because I couldn't read or jot down notes. I worked there for a year and a half. I was happy to get the pay and loved working with the children. I didn't earn a lot, but I remember when I worked from morning to midnight without *any* pay.

It was here that I met my first friends. People had a hard time understanding me, but I felt drawn right away to my boss, Liz, and two other women I worked with, Vickie and Annette. The short time we worked together—I worked there the longest out of us three—cemented our friendships, and to this day we still get together from time to time. I was assigned as a teacher's assistant, or TA, to work with Annette.

Annette

Annette and I seemed to connect right away. She understood my broken English pretty well, even over the phone. We both had a way of raising our voices when we became emotional. At times, it sounded as if we were screaming back and forth at each other. She was more laid back than I was. I was so used to working, working, working so I wouldn't get yelled at, so it was hard for me at first to slow down and be social as I did my work. I would complete a task and then hurry to get the next one done. Annette would say, "Slow down, Shari, relax. It'll get done. You don't have to work yourself to death." I had been so isolated for so long, even with people all around me, that I didn't yet have the social skills for interacting with others on the job. I was always in the background, invisible, and now I had to learn how to be just a regular person, working a job. It hadn't dawned on me this was an issue until I started working with Annette.

I got along so well with Annette, and at the time she lived so close to the preschool like I now did, that she'd often ask me if I wanted to take a walk with her. She didn't have her driver's license then, and of course I didn't drive, so walking was a part of life for us both.

My Name is Shari Ho

One day after work, we went on a long walk. It was then I got up the nerve to tell her my story. "Annette," I said, "I tell you something, okay?" We kept up a good pace as we strode down the sidewalk away from the preschool. I saw her wave at another coworker who had just pulled out of the parking lot and drove past us on the street. "Good for you guys! Walk off those pounds," the driver joked as Annette shouted back. Then she turned her attention back to me. "Go ahead," she replied. "Okay, I tell you my story." I took a deep breath and continued, "I was slave in Taiwan to Old Lady. I sold to her when I only seven. Came to U.S. and run away from her." Annette was oddly quiet while my incredible story came spilling out of me in short, choppy words. I repeated most of the phrases I knew over and over again, hoping to convey a deeper meaning with the few words I did know. So often human trafficking involves prostitution, abuse, and even rape, so I think Annette wasn't sure if she should ask me details about what happened, in case these horrible had things occurred. But she listened intently, and I felt her concern for me in the silence.

I can't tell you how good it felt to tell her the truth about myself! I had to know if she would feel the same about me after I told her, if she would still want to be my friend. Now the wondering was over, and she was still there with me. I don't remember how she reacted exactly. I do know that when I got to the part about how I escaped, she blurted out, "Oh my gosh! That is SO crazy!"

Most people don't really know what to say when they find out what happened to me. A few react with, "Wow! I can't believe this happened to you!" or "Oh, my goodness," or even, "I'm so sorry this happened." I understand how incredible this may seem. You can't always tell from the outside what someone has gone through on the inside.

Revealing my past to Annette gave me the strength to tell my boss, Liz, my story, too, who in turn told Vickie, so those in my closest circle at work learned my story, and they all made a huge effort, wanting to help me whenever they could.

Vickie

Vickie often took me shopping. We'd go to the grocery store, and we'd walk up and down the aisles. Vickie didn't rush me. She wanted me to enjoy the task and make decisions. She'd help me read different signs and stuff and then when we got to the checkout, she'd help me to pay. Writing checks was still hard for me to do. Vickie tried to teach me. "You put the date here and then write the amount there," she pointed with her finger, "then you have to spell out the amount on this line, as well." Most of the time she'd end up writing the amount in, and I would just sign my name below. She'd even go with me to the bank sometimes when I needed help.

I remember going make-up shopping with her. Both Vickie and Annette would tease me about my "expensive tastes." Living with The Old Lady and her daughter, who were so particular about what they wore and how they looked, and then living with Judy and her extravagant lifestyle, made me desire finer things, especially when I had been deprived of even my most basic needs for so long.

"Hey, wanna go to Walgreens on Saturday?" Vickie asked one day. "They have a big selection of make-up, and the prices are pretty cheap." "Vickie, you so good with money, listen to husband all time, you more Asian than me!" I replied with a smile. She laughed, and we made the date. Saturday came, and Vickie pulled up to the house. "Ready?" she called to me as I came out. I couldn't wait.

"What about this color?" Vickie suggested, pulling out a few different shades of eye shadow from the display on the wall. "Oooo ... " I said, as I reached my hand out towards the green one. "I love, love, love green one!" I said, almost giggling. This was so much fun! I was shopping for make-up with my friend. We must have spent hours going through all the eye shadow, lipstick, and nail polish. There were so many pretty colors. "Hey Shari, I want you to have this one. My treat," Vickie offered. She put the pretty green eyeshadow I had "oooed" at earlier in the basket, then headed to the register and set the items on the counter. The lady rung them up and put them in a bag. "Thank you for shopping at Walgreens," the clerk said, as we turned to walk out. I put my hand on Vickie's shoulder, and she turned to look at me. "Thank you. Thank you so much," I said, looking in her eyes with meaning. Yes, of course I was thankful for the make-up, but what I really wanted to say was, "Thank you for being my friend. Thank you for 'girl time,' being silly, being so 'normal' like girlfriends do; it means a lot to me."

Money, Shopping, and Me

I really didn't know how to budget, so money went fast. There were so many new things I needed to learn, and I just had to figure it all out on my own.

I only worked with really little kids, so I didn't learn much from them; co-workers would often point out, "You don't know how to spell that?" and they would help me. Spelling was hard for me. They would help me write. I had to fill out paperwork for my job; not everyone knew my story, but everyone was very helpful towards me.

Life On My Own

One day I was in a hurry, and Annette asked me why. "I have to go, walk dog." I usually walked home from time to time to walk Elsa's dog on my lunch break. Annette looked me in the eyes and said, "You know, you are free now, you don't have to do that." I guess I'd felt like I had to; after all, Elsa let me stay there. We talked about other things that I could do rather than live where I was now. I looked at her, and it was like a light went on inside. "I remember when I got out on my own," Annette continued. "I lived with a bunch of roommates. It was kind of crowded, but it was a lot of fun, and pretty cheap. Why don't we look in the paper and see if we can find a room for you to rent, maybe close by, so you can still walk to work?" I remember thinking, "What a great friend! I am so thankful that God has given me such a good friend in Annette."

So I found a place to rent with roommates on 23rd Street. The rent was $635 a month. It was for just a room with a shared living room, bathroom, and kitchen with several other roommates.

The guy renting it seemed nice, so I took it. I didn't have a bed so I saved up for one. I was now truly on my own.

The Nightmares

I was so very tired. I was going through so much emotionally at the time that I was finding it very hard to sleep. I'd be afraid to go to bed at night, wondering if somehow I'd be sent back to that family, forced to live with them again. I never told Elsa about the dreams nor the stress I carried. I pretended everything was okay. Living with this stress made our relationship difficult, and she seemed a little upset when I told her that I was moving out. I think she really did understand. She just wanted the best for me.

I began having these dreams—nightmares really—where I would see that Old Lady's angry face and hear her calling me names, telling me, "No one wants you; no one will ever want you, you worthless girl! I gave you a place to stay when no one would, and you treat me like this?! You thief and whore! I know who you really are inside ... you are a slave ... you will always be a slave!"

I'd wake up sweating, and my heart would be pounding out of my chest. It only got worse, and I was starting to have these same feelings during the day, too. I didn't know what was happening to me. Then, on the one-year anniversary of my escape, something frightening happened.

August 18, 2006

"Happy Birthday, Shari!" a co-worker said one day. I had told

171

everyone that although I didn't know my real birthday, the day I escaped my life of slavery would be my new birthday from now on. I had never celebrated a birthday in my life before, so I made a determined effort that this day would always be a big day to me. However, as special as I wanted that day to be, I was struggling with anxiety and was feeling pretty bad. "Let's go out and celebrate! We'll get a cake and everything," my friends said. I smiled and said, "Yeah, yeah, thank you!" but I felt so strange inside. I was there, but I wasn't there at the same time. We all met at a local restaurant, and we ate, and I got presents. The best part was when they all sang, "Happy Birthday!" and I blew out the candles on the cake. I forced myself to appear happy, which I was, but something was just not right.

As the evening wound down, I felt physically worse. When all but the last few friends left, I admitted to them that I felt so ill I needed to go to the hospital. "Are you okay? What's going on?" my closest friends asked. I told them all what had been happening to me lately—the nightmares, how my heart would race so fast I could barely breathe. I was having all of these symptoms now. I felt dizzy, and I had broken out in a cold sweat. Then, as I was explaining all this to them, my hands suddenly went numb. My chest tightened in pain, and my face turned pale. I thought I was going to die! This is when my friends became extremely concerned. They rushed me to the hospital immediately.

The Diagnosis

"Can you breathe in deeply for me?" the ER doctor asked. "How long have you had these symptoms?" He had a small light he flashed into my eyes, and it made me feel sick as he did it. "Can I ask if you have been under any stress lately?" He wrapped a band around my arm, and it quickly filled with air, pinching the skin on my arm tight. The anxiety was so overwhelming, I had trouble answering the questions. I was finally able to tell him some of my story. "Oh ... I see ... well, your heart looks fine ... " his voice trailed off. He had done other tests and after the nurse came in with the results, he studied them carefully. Then he turned his attention back to me and concluded, "Your heart looks normal ... no elevated levels that I can see ... hum ... I think these symptoms you are having are possibly panic attacks, or classic symptoms of what we call PTSD, or post-traumatic stress disorder. Usually, this occurs in people who have been through some pretty bad experiences for an extended period of time, like what you've just told me you have been through. You're not having a heart attack or anything. I can prescribe something for it, something that can help calm you down, but you're going to need to get some help dealing with all this." He scribbled something on a pad of paper he had, tore it off, and handed it to me. I couldn't read what was on it anyway, so I thought I would show it to my therapist the next day. He was a psychiatrist and had already given me some prescription Tylenol PM to help with my sleeplessness.

Therapy

Amy had arranged for me to see a therapist on a regular basis to help deal with the emotional trauma I had gone through. It was a struggle to find the right one and to feel comfortable sharing all of what I'd gone through. The therapist I had been seeing had a session available that next day, so I told him what had happened at the birthday party and what medicine the ER doctor had prescribed.

"Yeah, this should help calm you down. You should take this regularly," he said. "It does have some side effects, so you'll let me know if you experience any changes, will you?" He scribbled some notes down on a paper and asked a few more questions before I left. The medicine did make me feel less stressed, but I began having other feelings that I did not realize at first were side effects. I felt heavy and less coordinated. I began struggling to remember things at work. My deeper fears grew slowly stronger. I couldn't explain it, but I didn't like taking this drug, so I stopped. I continued to take the Tylenol PM, though. Without it, I couldn't sleep.

Saying Goodbye

"Beep, beep," the alarm screamed as I stepped through the security gate at the courthouse. Amy wanted me to go with her to meet someone there. "I think it's your belt, miss," the guard said as he waved a large, bat-shaped wand over my waist. "We'll need you to remove it." This became so crazy because the belt was sown into my pants, and I couldn't take it off! After some convincing, Amy managed to get us both through security in time to make our appointment.

"Shari, this is Lucy. She is an awesome case manager who'll help you with whatever you still need." Amy introduced me to this young woman who was close to my size and height. Amy was very tall and towered over us both. I felt sad, but also a little angry inside that Amy was leaving. I didn't know this woman, and she was going to be my new case manager. Why did Amy have to leave me when I still needed her?

Amy had done such wonderful work with the Task Force, but when the opportunity came for her to move to East Africa to be an Aftercare Fellow with the International Justice Mission in Kampala Uganda and then to process refugees for the U.S. refugee resettlement based out of Nairobi Kenya, she couldn't pass it up. Deep inside, I knew she had to go, and I was ready to let her go—I just didn't want to admit it.

Lucy

Lucy was very different from Amy. Where Amy was outgoing and vocal, Lucy was more reserved and quiet. She was strong and a fighter, though, and she would be there for me no matter what, just like Amy had been. Lucy was also of Asian descent, so I felt an immediate connection to her.

In 2006, Lucy was working with the Victim Witness Program, a part of CSP, as a supervisor. She was new to the program but already had a heavy caseload, mostly domestic violence cases. She worked with the DA's office, handling everything from domestic violence to vehicular manslaughter. I was to be her first human trafficking survivor. With her experience and background, this job would be both old and new to her. I have to admit that I cried that day. I didn't know how I would ever trust Lucy to be my case man-

175

ager, but in time she would become very special to me.

Lucy was deeply serious about what she did. "I think, with a trafficking survivor, one of the most important things we can do is to give them choices," she once said in an interview. She worked with me, helping me to create more options in my life. When she could, she would introduce me to others who could help as well. This is when I met another wonderful friend, Sister Marianna.

Sister Marianna

"I understand you would like to learn to read English?" she asked me in Chinese as we sat across from one another. Sister Marianna was a Catholic nun with the Sisters of St. Joseph. She had begun volunteering time with the HTTF after her training in New York. Her focus was education, especially helping those who were victims of human trafficking. She had been a nun for over thirty years. She was born in Hong Kong and had been living in Canada when she felt the calling to serve God as a nun. Lucy knew I wanted to get a driver's license, but reading English was still so difficult for me, so she paired me with Sister Marianna for tutoring. Since Sister Marianna spoke Mandarin, which I also spoke, it was a perfect match.

"I'd like to record some of the lessons with you, Shari, if you don't mind. I can use them, perhaps, to teach others," Sister Marianna said. She was a logical and very practical woman. She rarely let emotion keep her from what she thought was best for me, and from the moment we met, we developed a caring and trusting relationship. I was always on her mind when she'd receive donations, in case I had any needs that weren't being met. So many times when I needed help financially, her wonderful students raised the money I needed.

God

At first, Sister Marianna and I didn't talk about God. She taught me about letters and the sounds they made. I even began to write a little. Our lessons would be on and off again because of both our schedules. One day I said, "I can't meet that day, I have to go to church." This opened a door, and slowly we talked more and more about God.

I started sharing what I was praying about with Sister Marianna. "I think I want God to help me find my family someday," I told her. She would always smile at what I said, but she would also be very practical in her advice. "And how will you go about doing this?" she asked. She always challenged me. She never let me say something without asking my plan, making me think. She was always honest and straightforward. She never lied or let me get away with anything. I loved this.

I remember once after she had helped me with reading the DMV materials, she was supposed to take me home. "We stop at Target to buy card? It Mother's Day. I want to give lady who help me escape card," I asked.

There were so many cards to choose from, and they all had such pretty pictures on them, but I had no idea what they said.

"You read to me so I know what it say," I asked. She read them all and then I chose the one that I really liked. It was pretty expensive, but perfect. Sister Marianna, being Chinese, suggested, "Why not buy this pack of blank cards and copy the nice saying on to one of them?" There was a McDonald's inside the store. I bought the pack of cards and sat at a table. I looked at the card and after a minute or two I said, "How can I copy this? There no line for me to keep words straight." Sister Marianna went and got a napkin and placed the edge in such a way I could use it as a ruler of sorts. It took me about twenty minutes to write it out but I did it. She was a good teacher!

Whenever I needed advice or help, I would call Sister Marianna. She has remained a good friend and protector of mine. God brought her to me at the right time.

Chapter 14

The Date

A friend at work asked me one day, "Do you have a boyfriend?" I shyly answered, "No." All those years as a slave I had never been allowed to make contact with anyone, let alone men. "I have a friend. We went to school together, and I've known him a long time. We grew up together," she explained, "He's a nice guy." She took a picture of me with her phone. At that time, I was skinny, and my face had broken out with pimples. I was probably a hundred pounds and wore no make-up. "There," she pushed send on her phone. "If he asks, can I give him your phone number?" She said all this as if it was no big deal to her. I answered nervously and burst out with, "Okay, I don't care," hoping to end the awkward conversation. I thought to myself that this must be a joke; she is only kidding. Who could like me? I had always been told that no one would ever want me, and if I ever did marry, I would be caught in an endless cycle of marriages and divorces. "You are of no real use to anyone," The

Old Lady's voice echoed in my mind. I shrugged off my co-worker's words and went back to work.

A week later, I was surprised to get a call from Derrick. It wasn't much of a call. Through the language barrier the only word I recognized in the conversation was "dinner," and I just repeated it back to him. On Friday, Derrick came and picked me up. He was a big guy, strong and gentle. Sister Marianna would later call him a big teddy bear. With dark hair and a light complexion, he towered over me. Well, most people tower over me, but Derrick's build was not intimidating. He introduced himself. I saw a kindness in his eyes that drew me to him. I always look in a person's eyes when I meet them, and in his I felt safe and unafraid.

Dinner and a Movie

I grabbed my purse, and we headed out the door to his car. There was a BJ's Bar and Grill not too far from where I lived at the time, so Derrick asked if it was okay to go there. My answer to most things was, "Okay, I don't care," so I repeated that to him. We found a place to park and walked towards the restaurant. The place was packed. It was a Friday night, and people buzzed around like bees, hoping to find a place to eat and forget about the work week. We waited about thirty minutes before I heard, "Derrick, party of two. Derrick?" We followed our server to a booth. All the while, I just smiled and nodded my head to whatever he said. There were TVs on every wall blaring baseball, basketball, hockey, or whatever sport might be playing that night. It was odd, but all the sounds felt

The Date

soothing to me. "I am just an ordinary girl out on an ordinary date," I told myself. I was sitting across from a strange man, yet somehow I felt comfortable with him. I don't think the waiter understood our date. I looked so very young with a nervous break-out of pimples dotting my face. He kept coming over to check on us, or rather, me. We must have looked like a strange couple—this big, tall, white guy and a skinny, teenage-looking Asian. You could count the words that were said between us. I wondered what Derrick was thinking. I couldn't read at all, so he had to read the menu to me and explain each item, pointing to the pictures from time to time. My friends were always correcting my English, and they must've told Derrick that, because he was doing it, too. I didn't mind. In fact, I liked it!

For most people, a blind date can be filled with many awkward moments, but I didn't feel that way with Derrick. I could tell he liked me as much as I liked him. Most of our dinner continued in silence with a few attempts at small talk, me hacking away at English and Derrick responding with "Yeah, uh ... like, you know, uh kinda, yeah, uh ... good." After we had finished he asked, "You up for a movie? There is a theatre here, and we could see if there is something we both like." I was happy that he was interested enough in me to want to keep the evening going. We approached the ticket booth, and he read all the movie choices out loud. "Hey, look!" He pointed towards the marquee at one of the titles, "*Crouching Tiger, Hidden Dragon* is playing. Wanna do it? And what luck, it's in Chinese!"

181

I don't know if that was planned, but I could understand the movie perfectly. Later, I would find that Derrick was a huge fan of anything Kung Fu and especially Jet Li. Then we drove over to his friend's house and visited until nearly midnight. Well, Derrick visited while I mostly giggled and smiled, trying to look like I understood what they were saying.

My First Real Boyfriend

It was pretty late when we got back to my place. I was nervous, but I liked him a lot. He walked me to the door, but he didn't try to touch me or to kiss me. He said, "Good night," and watched me go inside and close the door. I felt safe.

I was happy inside. I knew he was interested, but he took things pretty slow, not wanting to rush things, which made me trust him, really trust him. What if he found out what has happened to you? Will he still want to be with you then? My thoughts echoed what The Old Lady might say, "No one will want you! No one!" But I was too happy at this moment to think on such things. I went inside to the little room I had rented, closed the door, and went to bed.

I continued to date Derrick, and it became a steady thing. We went out two to three times a week. This was a time of transition for me, as I became a real person with a job and a boyfriend, as I tried to sever the past and get the justice I deserved. I felt like a rubber band, being pulled and stretched, twisted and sometimes extended beyond what I thought I could take. It was exciting and petrifying all at the same time. I had decided to let Derrick in on my past. We had been together for a few months and I thought, maybe, the weight of my past would not be as heavy if he was there to help carry it with me. Expressing myself was difficult, but I knew the word, 'slave,' and with the coaching of my case manager, I managed to explain things to Derrick. Whether he understood completely at that time or not, he seemed to take it well. He didn't ask many questions, and although my words were limited, he was a man of few words himself. Confident that I could now talk freely and have a shoulder to cry on, our relationship continued— slowly, which I was so very thankful for—but steadily.

Fire and Ice

Derrick and I were so different. I was very quiet and shy when we first started going out, but as I began to see things in Derrick that bothered me, I got pretty feisty with him. He liked to drink and party, and many of our dates ended at one of his friend's houses with everybody drinking and me sitting there, unable to communicate with anyone. I was beginning to hate these dates. "Take me home," I'd say after several hours. Derrick would drive me home and then return to the party for more drinking. We were starting to get into arguments, and they were pretty heated ones.

Once, I threw a plate across the room. I wasn't trying to hit Derrick, I was just so frustrated, and I couldn't say what I wanted to say. I was angry, so throwing something got that idea across. "Calm down," he'd say, "I don't know what else you want from me, Shari;

this is just who I am." This relationship was a constant tug-of-war. We both wanted different things from each other, and we were lousy at communicating it.

Derrick never fought back. He never pushed back. It was a good thing. It was a bad thing, too.

My 'Evil Godmother'

It was always me pushing, trying to move things ahead and find a life for us, but it seemed Derrick was always on pause, slowing things down, keeping us stuck. He was a big, soft teddy bear, and just as lifeless when I needed him the most. We were just two good people who were so very bad together. After a big fight, I did what I usually did: I called Sister Marianna. Most people, when they are hurting, reach out to a friend who brings comfort and warmth, who generously doles out plenty of, "Ahh ... that's too bad ... " or "Yeah, what a jerk!" Sister Marianna was not that friend. "Look, you know how Derrick is, you knew this when you got involved with him. Why cry when it won't change things?" Sister Marianna always told the truth, even when it hurt. But that was the very thing I needed from her. I didn't need to feel sorry for myself. For too many years I had felt sad and helpless; I never wanted to feel that way again. "Let's talk about what you are going to do about this," she began. And talk we did. She would give me as much time as I needed, sometimes talking to both Derrick and me while we were in the middle of a fight. Talking us down off the ledge was her specialty, but it was not sweet-talking. She'd often say, "I feel like an evil godmother to you two."

So many times Derrick and I were on the brink of breaking up and didn't. He was my first love, and I so desperately wanted him to be everything to me, and he just couldn't be. I was changing so much at the time. That stubborn opinionated girl was being reborn, and at times she was just out of control. Facing my past put my emotions in high gear.

I don't think Derrick really knew how to handle all of this either. Our relationship was still new and just telling him about being a survivor was difficult to do.

I didn't realize then that this would be a long and painful relationship.

Disturbing Changes

"Ahhh ... " I held my head in my hands because it just hurt so much. I had been screaming at Derrick, throwing things and feeling out of control. I couldn't understand what was happening to me. Sometimes I felt like I was flying into a rage for no reason at all; other times I would fall apart in tears and cry for hours. I was having more and more panic attacks, which had terrible physical symptoms as well. This frightened me. "Am I normal?" I asked my therapist during a session one afternoon. "Shari, this is all a part of your PTSD. What you are experiencing is normal. Many things can trigger it: a smell, a look, a dream, how someone treats you. It can be difficult, as hard as you try, to turn it off. As you begin to work through things, the symptoms can be managed. We can try some other medications that may help."

I didn't feel normal. I felt hopeless. I didn't want to take any medicine; everything I tried made me feel so much worse. It was hard to keep going every day. Anger and depression flipped back and forth like a switch. But mostly, I started to feel like I didn't want to live anymore.

As I walked out of that session and into the sunlight, I was in a daze. I could not feel the warmth of the sun nor hear the traffic in the street or the sounds of people laughing, hurrying down the sidewalk. The world was silent, grey, and tasteless. The pain of knowing that this was how it was always going to be was overwhelming. What was the purpose of fighting anymore? Why resist any longer? I still felt like that little girl, looking out of the window, searching the faces of those passing by on the street for the familiar one that would take me away from my nightmare—my mom, my dad—who promised to come take me home. Instead, I heard The Old Lady constantly reminding me, "Your family sold you to *me*; they will not come to take you home. This is your home now." I saw the cars racing past. "Woosh. Zoom." I felt the stream of air from their movement blow hot air onto my face. "It can end so easily right here," my mind tempted. "Keep on walking, those cars won't have time to stop. You won't even feel it." I walked slowly and purposefully, edging ever closer to the busy drivers, who were focused

The Date

on their journey home, who had lives they looked forward to and rushed to meet. The gusts from the speed of the vehicles passing me pulled at the sleeves of my sweater. I kept walking mindlessly. Did anyone notice? Did anyone care? I saw no faces, only blurs of light and color as I walked on, ever closer to the street. "Deet do dee detta leet," my cell phone called loudly and repeated endlessly, forcing me to wake up from this zombie walk I had begun. I hadn't realized how deep in my thoughts I had been. I was standing in the street, inches away from a car that swerved around me, and as I reached into my purse to find my phone, a loud blast from the driver's horn made my heart jump—nearly causing me to drop the phone. I quickly stepped back up on the curb. "Oh ... ahh ... I mean, hello?" I managed to say. It was my friend Liz, whom I hadn't heard from in a while. "Shari, I just had to call you. I couldn't wait!"

Thank God for her call! What news she had I don't remember, but the good news was that it saved my life. I cannot tell of all of the times God was there with me in those terrible moments to rescue me.

Part V
Fighting to Stay Free

Chapter 15

Facing the Past

W e'll need to get a deposition from you, Shari, your side of the story. It'll be recorded in front of the lawyers from both sides. The Family will be there as well..." my lawyer's voice trailed off. *The Family will be there!* My thoughts screamed this so loudly, I thought I had actually spoken it. I felt a sick pit in my stomach as I finally formed the words, my voice cracking as I blurted, "I can't—" I gathered strength. "I do NOT want to be in same room with those... those people!" The whole tone in the room changed. I heard, "It's okay," and, "Don't worry, we'll be with you," but I couldn't shake the nausea and horrible fear that gripped me. I knew I had to do this, that going to court would finally happen, but all the thoughts of seeing The Daughter again, of her staring at me, and the memories of what she had done to me were still so real, and this new life of freedom seemed so unreal, I had to shut my thoughts off or I knew I would want to run and hide. The true me inside was fighting too hard to let that happen.

"Shari, this is how we will show them that you are no longer a slave to them," my lawyer explained. "They have no power over you anymore; they will be there, doing the same as you, giving their side of the story. It will be a difficult thing to face, but you can. You will be able to do it."

She's Not There

The thought of having to face The Daughter and her husband stayed with me all that day. I knew The Old Lady would not be there at the deposition. I had a slight feeling of sadness as I remembered hearing that she had been so shaken when I escaped (and the fact she was over 90 years old) that The Daughter had put her into a home. She didn't live long after that. I had only been free a year when I heard she had died in that convalescent home, alone. In my last days with her, she had gradually gotten more unpredictable and paranoid and would often lash out at me for no reason, accusing me of ridiculous things, calling me "two-faced" and beating me with a cane saying, "I know you, you thief and lying thing, you listen to what I say and tell *her* everything!" speaking of her daughter. I had known then that her mind must be going and felt sorry for that, but her words still hit me just as hard as her cane did. This "grandma" had been nothing but cruel to me, always. She was dead now. It should be all over, but it wasn't. No, she wouldn't be there physically, but I still saw her angry face in my dreams.

Facing the Past

Court Deposition

This was the first time I had seen The Daughter since I had escaped that August night when Judy sped us away in the dark. I couldn't sleep the night before. I kept seeing their faces and hearing the horrible things they had said to me: "You're a worthless whore! No one wanted you, no one will ever want you, you stupid girl!"

A doctor I had been seeing had prescribed some anxiety pills, so I took half a tablet like he had told me to do. It helped a little, yet I still tossed and turned all night. The next morning, I was still so overwhelmed with the thought of all that had happened to me and the prospect of facing my captors that I took a whole pill after breakfast and waited for Lucy to pick me up. The deposition was scheduled for around 10 a.m., and the drive was not very far. I thought I would wait outside the house, hoping the fresh cool air and morning sun might give me a bit of relief and a measure of peace. How could I face that woman again? I just wanted my thoughts to be miles away from the hell I endured all those years. Up until now, I could never tell them no or speak freely without the fear that some terrible consequence—physical or verbal—would be unleashed on me. I had started a new life and did not want to see them reaching their hands back into it. They had always won in the past, would they win again? Would the truth ever justify me?

"Hey, I'm not late am I?" Lucy called out as she approached me. I was so lost in my thoughts I hadn't seen her car pull up to the curb. "You okay?" she asked, looking at me, concerned. My hair was pulled back in a ponytail, and I was wearing a long-sleeved black shirt. I think I must've looked like my best friend had died, as I had the most serious look on my face. "I'm okay," I lied, but I knew she didn't believe me. "You can do this, Shari. You are strong—stronger than they are. You have made it so far. You won't be alone in this. We are all with you." Her encouraging words held me together as I got in the car. It seemed just moments, and we were there.

The boardroom where we met was filled with people: lawyers, interpreters, recorders. I purposefully set my gaze away from The Old Lady's Daughter, who was sitting across the table towards my left. She sat next to her husband. I swear all I could hear was my head pounding like it was going to explode at any moment. I swallowed in a deep breath as we began. "Let's all state our names..."

I said my name, but I really didn't hear what I was saying. My deadpan face was turned to the side, fixed in an emotionless gaze. "Yes, that is my name," the high-pitched voice of The Old Lady's Daughter responded as she took her turn at introductions. My stomach was tied in knots as I heard that voice—a sound I hadn't heard in a long time. I had but a moment to think about that before the questions started. Question after question bombarded me. The lawyers asked the same questions over and over again, and no matter how I answered them, they weren't acceptable because the lawyer would just ask them again.

I refused to look in the direction of The Daughter. I would not acknowledge her; I knew I must stay strong and not allow her to enter my eyes, to gain power over me again; I refused to be afraid.

Facing the Past

I felt that every question was designed to force me to show my weaknesses. "Have you ever seen a doctor? What medications are you on? Why were you taken to the hospital? How much money do you make an hour? If you didn't want to do something that you were told to do, why didn't you just tell them no?" All the while, The Daughter heard every detail: my friends' names, where I lived and worked, personal information about my anxiety, and the medication I must take to calm my thoughts. I grew more and more angry with every question until I finally burst out in broken English, "I'm just trying to remember everything you ask me, and every time I answer it the wrong way ... I don't want ... I want ... if you ask me, I want true, everything true. I want to say everything true. Because there are so many questions I say, yes, no, no, okay? I'm sorry. Why you want to find my friends? They know my story, they know what's true. Find them then. Okay? I not trying to hide anything from you, I not lie, they know; we are fine, we are happy."

I didn't know if I was making any sense at all but the repetition of the same questions, the constant, "What is their last name? Where do they live?" regarding my friends, felt like The Daughter was being given permission to harass them and ruin my new life. Then, when they began to interrogate me about The Old Lady, who I had called Grandma, and asked, "Did you ever object to calling her Grandma?" I burst out again. "DON'T! Please, don't. This ... she is NOT my grandma! Can you call her lady? You say always ... because you always say grandma. Can you change that? Just call her lady or call her by her name. She NOT my grandma!" The frustration on my face made me feel flushed. I looked back and

195

forth, trying hard not to set my eyes on *her*. I was so very angry. I felt attacked. But it made the fighter in me come out. No one spoke out for me, so I would have to now.

Breaking Free

When I look back at this moment, I see how important it was. The Old Lady was NOT my grandmother. She was NOT someone who could or should ever have held that title with me. She was never pleased with me, and she never loved me. I didn't know it then, but I was surgically removing that woman from my heart.

"Tell us, ah, how did you come to the U.S.? What happened?" I told them everything. I held nothing back. The Daughter just sat there, looking like she had no idea what I was talking about, trying to look so innocent. As I got to the part where I got so sick when my legs were infected, I felt like a volcano inside, my words exploding, sharp and forceful.

"This was very hard time for me. My legs ... so painful ... swollen ... nothing would fit me. No wear shoes ... no wear pants. Even neighbors, people ... shocked at how swollen ... told The Old Lady and her daughter I should see doctor ... they wouldn't take me. Two week passed before they took me to see doctor. Even he afraid to touch my legs. I see his face—he didn't want to touch me, afraid of the sores ... I could not believe I was treated like this!" Suddenly, I looked directly at The Daughter, my face determined as I fired away at her with my words, "How could you treat me like this? You can still sit there, with that smirk on your face, knowing how painful this was for me!" I guess that was enough for the lawyers. They asked that we take a break and for me to take some time to cool down. Oh, how angry I was that they were getting away with treating me so terribly!

Pushed to the Edge

The break didn't change much. Things continued as they had been before with question after question. Sometimes my answers came with anger, sometimes tears, but the lawyers for The Daughter showed no concern or compassion. After my life was cut open there in front of them all, the question finally came, "You said earlier, something about being suicidal. What did you mean by that?" I gathered my thoughts and gripped myself from the inside, for I felt the tears beginning to form, and I hated for The Old Lady's Daughter to see them. "Because I was thinking of it a lot," I finally began, "I was thinking about many, many things. When I wanted to escape and when I escaped, I thought about all of the things that happened back then. That's it. Just many things I was thinking about in my mind. Of course, naturally, I would be thinking about suicide." The lawyer could not let that answer be enough and pursued it further, "You say 'naturally,' why do you say 'naturally' you would be thinking about suicide?" I could not control the tears as they began to fill my eyes, and I continued to let the pain flow out in that cold and uncaring boardroom. The Old Lady's Daughter sat there, unmoved. The lawyers, unbelieving and as cold as the room, rifled through their papers. My lawyer sat near me, but I felt no comfort or strength from anyone as I began again to explain. "I think about many things, because I was very sad. I thought about

197

my grandmother—but she is not my grandmother. I thought about when I was little. I thought about how badly she treated me. She did not treat me like a family, she did not treat me like a granddaughter. Whatever I did she was always displeased. I will not forget. What I will never, ever be able to forget is Grandmother, judging me and my family, because we had nothing to eat, so she would accuse me of stealing food, stealing things to eat. This 'grandmother' would beat me with whatever she could find near her: a bamboo rod, a hanger, her cane. She would hit me and say horrible things to me, cursing me, telling me I would have been nothing if she did not buy me."

The pain, the heart-wrenching emotion of being so unloved and uncared for forced the tears to flow down my face, stinging my cheeks and chin. I pulled a tissue from a small plastic pack that sat on the large table in front of me. I wiped the salty streaks as the memories poured back into my mind. I was almost there again, with that Old Lady, with The Daughter, hearing and feeling the abuse. I waited for the translator to finish conveying my painful thoughts. "What I can never forget, what I will never be able to forget, is one time The Old Lady accused me of stealing and drinking some of her ginseng tea. I was doing my chores, cleaning the kitchen when she went into a rage. 'I paid good money to your father, to your family, and for what? Now you steal from me! You disgusting thief!' I had not stolen anything from her; I would never steal. She grabbed my head and pulled it back, gripping my hair in her hands and pulling it hard. She refused to let me go. I struggled, but I was so very small, and she was very strong. She dragged me by my hair, down the hall towards the bathroom." Uncontrollably, my voice grew tight and tears streamed down my face, my lips tasting the bitter drops as I forced myself to reveal this abusive act. "She, this 'grandmother' of mine, pulled me onto the floor and snatching the filthy brush used to clean the toilet, she stuffed it into my mouth. I was not a human being to her and never would be. I had wanted her to love me like a granddaughter, but she treated me worse than a dog on the street. Yes, my mother sold me, but even she would not treat me like this. I missed my mama so much then." I knew the lawyer would not let me continue much longer but I had to let everyone know how horrible The Old Lady had been, how terribly they all had treated me and how they were now trying to turn my words, all this, into lies. I could not let this happen, so I continued on, "I remember The Old Lady would only feed me food that was already spoiled and refused to let me sit at the table but forced me to eat in a corner like a mongrel. I thought a lot about trying to leave and find my mother, but how? I did not know where she was or how to find her. It was a constant flow of abuse, both physical with beatings and emotional with the harsh words and cursing. I never knew what I did wrong to deserve this."

I was done. I spoke out the unspeakable to The Daughter's face. I let the lawyers know. The truth was recorded on video, transcribed, undeniable. As I pulled more tissues out of the pack, the plastic crinkled loudly in the silent room. I wiped my eyes, lips, and nose from the wetness of my tears.

The lawyer for The Old Lady's Daughter was unmoved. He

even chuckled as he responded, "You've gone on a lot ... I'm not sure it was even in response to my question." My lawyer chimed in, "You asked her about her suicidal thoughts ... " "I did," he replied, but he just had to put a dig in there, not realizing his words stabbed at my already wounded heart. "And I'm not sure the long narrative was responsive, but ... " I cut him off, as now my tears had dried, and anger rose up in me. "Well, that's my answer. Every time I thought about these things, it caused me a lot of pain," I fired back. He tried to soften his callousness and started again with, "I ..." But I jumped in again. "No, I wanted to explain. I understand what you asked me. Why was I suicidal? This was the only thought I had, to terminate myself; take my own life. You do not know the experiences that I have gone through, if you had, you would not be able to answer all these questions. It would be hard for you; maybe you would understand what I felt."

Seed Sown

A few minutes of silence passed while the lawyer took a few breaths and then continued his questioning, without acknowledging my tears or pain. "You only *thought* about suicide? Did you physically take any steps to kill yourself?" "I wanted to jump off a building, take sleeping pills, but I didn't. Now there are people in my life that do care about me, and I thought about them, but the memories of living with The Old Lady, trapped with her and her daughter day after day ... it haunts me still every day." I was mad as I said this, but it didn't stop them from asking the same questions again. "Did you *try* to kill yourself? Did you slit your wrists? Take too many pills? Jump off a building? Do any other stuff to actually try to go through with it?"

I am sure he was just trying to do his job, after all, he had to represent his client in court, but he spoke in such a sterile way, and he was almost mean at times. Did he wish me to reconsider suicide? A small voice egged me on, "Yeah, just thoughts, huh? I don't believe any of this. If it were true, why didn't you try?"

"Yes. Okay? Once I really thought about suicide. I was walking. I saw a vehicle, an oncoming car in the street, and so I stepped out into its path. I was still standing in the middle of the street when my cell phone suddenly rang. It was my friend, Liz. I snapped out of it and woke up as the vehicle swerved around me, honking as it went. Okay? Is this what you want? Okay?" More frustration and anger dried my tears as the lawyer once again ignored my words and went on to the next question.

They all wanted to paint a picture that I was not treated unfairly by The Old Lady or her daughter. They claimed I was given gifts, expensive jewelry, and that my life would have been no different had I not been living with them. And when I would explain my side, it seemed to get me nowhere. My life would have been no different?

"You shopped at Ross, right?" Of course, I went shopping with The Old Lady, I was her servant, her slave. Everywhere we went, she leaned her heavy bodyweight on my shoulder as if I were her cane. I carried her bags, waited on her hand and foot. I never

201

left her sight. I was not hanging out with her and shopping with my own money. I was not there of my own choice. I *had* to be there. Did they buy clothes for me? Yes, once or twice a year, but mostly I wore hand-me-downs given to me from the church. They had to keep up appearances. Buy me clothes? For three years I owned only three pairs of pants and one top. I hand-washed my clothes each night so I would at least be clean. Yet the interrogation went on and on.

When the lawyer continued to harass me about an expensive present of jewelry—a so-called gold watch—I lost it once again and spoke to The Daughter to her face. "Gold watch? Why you make up such stories? Never, never ever. You sit there making up lies. You have always fixed things to make you look like you are in the right, but God sees. He alone knows everything that happened throughout the years, as I do. I am so angry that even now you refuse to tell the truth. I took nothing with me that night that I escaped, nothing but the clothes on my back. I knew that anything that I had was really yours, so I refused to take it. But one thing that was given to me, not by you or your mother, but by a good woman from the church ... a Bible that means so much to me. I could not read it then and cannot yet now, but I know that the words that God speaks are in that book, and He is the reason I am here today; here, free from you and from The Old Lady that brought me so much harm and pain. It was He alone who watched over me, keeping me from hating. I only wanted to be loved and accepted into your family, but you would not have that. You lie here in front of us all, but He knows everything. God has seen it all." My anger had reached a point that I had to speak my mind to the lawyer as well, so when he tried to tell me I treated The Old Lady's Daughter to lunch, went shopping, and did other things of my own free will, I looked straight at him and said, "I worked for her ... The Daughter ... I had to go with The Old Lady. I did not do any of this because I wanted to. They calculated the time. If I came back late I would be grilled as to why. I couldn't speak English at all. Who could I talk to? Where could I go on foot that they couldn't find me? You hear my explanation and then say, 'I didn't ask you about the time, I didn't ask you about this or that' then you strike my answer from the record and say I am not responsive! I can no longer calm down. You continue to ask me questions only to want me to answer the way you want me to! I can no longer calm down."

It wasn't too long after this that we had to end and reschedule for another time to speak, but the damage had been done. I was angry and deeply emotional, and the flood of memories that I kept back in the dark every day had been set free to torment my mind. I was not okay after this. I felt completely hopeless, and I wasn't sure what I was going to do. I had sat there answering questions for over seven hours, and my energy was completely drained. I got up and left. Lucy was waiting outside the boardroom to drive me back home.

I Lost, They Won

I was SO depressed after leaving the deposition. My case manager, Lucy, was so supportive and caring, but I just couldn't express to her what was going on inside me. "You sure you're okay?" Lucy asked as she drove me back home. I sat in the car, looking out the window at all the traffic and people passing by in the street. The truth was all that mattered to me. All of those years, all of the things that happened to me—I spoke the truth. I faced The Old Lady's Daughter and I told the truth, but it didn't seem to make a difference. They always lied, and they always seemed to win. "I okay," I managed to squeeze out of my completely exhausted body. My throat felt sore from trying to keep from crying. I wanted to just break down and bawl, but I felt it would do no good now.

I lost. They won. They would always win, so what else was there?

"Are you *sure* you're okay? You'd tell me, right, if you weren't?" Lucy coaxed once more. "I mean, you gotta promise me if you're not okay you will tell me. Promise me. You gotta promise me, Shari, you'll call me if you're not okay." Still mindlessly staring out the window, I reassured her again, "Yeah ... okay ... I okay."

We arrived at my apartment after 8 p.m. As we said goodbye, I managed to stretch my lips into a half-hearted smile. "Thank you very much that you come today with me, Lucy. Thank you so much." I unbuckled my seatbelt and got out of the car. I didn't even turn around to see her drive away, I just turned and headed towards the door.

As I walked through the door, I could hear my landlord, who lived there with me and my other two roommates. He didn't hear me come in, and I was glad that I could just go to my room unnoticed. "Why is all this happening to me?" I cried out to God, my eyes too empty for tears, my heart so broken I could hardly get the words out. "I just told the truth. That is all I did, but still it doesn't seem to matter. They will continue to fight with me forever. How can they always win? I can't do this anymore." I saw the bottle of Tylenol PM that I had placed near my bed. How I just wanted to sleep, to forget this all, to be done with living this life.

I took the bottle. Then I went into the bathroom and filled a glass halfway with water. I shook the bottle. Plenty of pills rattled against the sides of the container. I didn't hesitate. I swallowed them all down with a mouthful or two of water. I mechanically opened a drawer and grabbed my razor. This was a bit harder for me to do, but I angled the disposable razor as best I could, pressing the metal blades against the soft skin of my wrist and jerking it quickly across. It stung, and I began to bleed.

My cell phone was lying on the bed. I looked at it, and for whatever reason, I called Lucy's office. "You've reached the voice-mail of ... " The message began, and I waited for the beep and said, "Thank you, Lucy, for everything. You helped me so much. Thank you." I hung up the phone and sat on the bed. I don't remember anything after that, but I know I didn't care anymore. The lawyer's words rang in my ears as he kept asking over and over, "You only *thought* about it, didn't you? But did you DO anything? Take any pills? Slit your wrists? Jump off a building? Did you do any other stuff to *actually* try to go through with it?" I guess I hadn't. It was as if the lawyer was calling me a liar, too! Well, it was the truth now.

Lucy had driven away, but I hadn't convinced her that I was really okay. She knew something was wrong. She was already late for another appointment, and when she arrived, the time seemed to drag on. I had no idea how troubled she was over my frame of mind. "Mind if I step out for a moment?" she asked. She checked her office voicemail and heard my voice saying, "Thank you, Lucy, for everything ... " There was something very wrong in those words. Lucy couldn't quite put her finger on it, but everything was not okay. She headed back towards my apartment, jumped out of the car, and walked up to the door. After a few knocks, the landlord answered the door. "Shari? Yeah, I dunno, she's probably here. She must be in her room." He motioned for Lucy to come in, and they walked towards my bedroom door. If she knocked at the door, I never heard her. The door was locked. I didn't hear her when she walked around the back to knock on my window, either.

An urgency rose up in Lucy she just couldn't explain. She left but drove around the block and came back to my place. "I know I was just here," she told the landlord, "but Shari's *got* to be here. I just called her boyfriend, and he said she wouldn't go anywhere on foot. Can you get the key and open her bedroom door?" The landlord hesitated before he said, "I'm not supposed to do that." Lucy quickly cut him off in mid-sentence, "Either unlock that door or I'll kick it in with my foot!" she demanded. Without a word, the landlord got the key and handed it to Lucy. "God, help Shari to be okay—"

Facing the Past

The door opened, and Lucy saw me lying across the bed, unresponsive. She could see by my wrists what I had been up to, and she called 911 as fast as she could. By this time, it was about two in the morning, and the paramedics arrived in the ambulance and transported me to the hospital. Lucy followed them in her car. Though I have no memory of it, Lucy stayed there in the ER with me until the pills had been flushed from my system, I was bandaged, and given a room. Derrick was out of town at the time, so Lucy called his mother, who also came and waited at the hospital. When I woke up, I found myself in a hospital bed with my robe and slippers on a chair near me. I thanked God that Lucy was there to save my life. I will always be thankful that she came back to check on me. I thank God every day for my life.

My Family of Friends

Lucy was not the only one who cared for me. I am so blessed to have a family of such wonderful friends. Although I have little memory of my hospital stay, I know Annette showed up for a visit because she had to tell me what happened when she came in the room. "Shari, Liz and I heard you were in the hospital and had to come see you right away," Annette explained. My boss, Liz, who was such a wonderful friend, had seen I had been struggling. She had even stayed over one night when I was feeling pretty depressed, sleeping on the floor, too concerned to leave. "If it's okay, let me stay over. I just want to make sure you're okay," she had pleaded. The girls at work could see things were bad. I was crying all the time. I had just started counseling, and during those sessions, the past came up. The counselor would have me draw pictures of the abuse. This had added to everything I was going through, and I just couldn't handle it all at the time.

I really didn't want anyone coming over at that time, but Liz had insisted. I didn't want to live anymore, so I think I scared the heck out of her.

"Liz and I were out having drinks the other night, and we got a call that you were in the hospital. We had to come to see how you were," Annette continued on. "You were just lying there, Shari, in the bed. You were so still, with bandages around your wrists. And then I saw you had this bandana on your head, you know, wrapped around your forehead. The word NUTS was written on it. I gasped and was thinking like, 'Oh, no! They think you're crazy!' I didn't realize it was an allergy alert—that you're allergic to nuts!" I burst out laughing. Annette laughed, too. I laughed so hard, tears rolled down my face. How could I ever feel like life is not worth living? I again remember my mother's words, "Today might be a bad day, but it will be better tomorrow." I would be in the hospital for a few more days and would find out not long after this that my struggle with this family was finally over. The case would be settled without me having to return to that boardroom again. There were still many bad days to come, but my past was steadily being put behind me for good, and for that, I will forever be thankful.

Chapter 16

Survivors Groups

As much as there was a victim in me, there was a fighter inside me, too. Since I was a little girl, I have always had an anger towards injustice. When my sister was given up for adoption, I was just seven years old, but I knew then that I was a fighter, and though many times I wouldn't fight for myself, that fighter was in there, waiting, growing stronger in spite of my circumstances.

Counseling is a big part of a survivor's recovery. Maybe that's what started the process of setting that fighter in me free. And just like anything or anyone that has been chained up for so long, when it's finally set free, it runs wild for a time. My feelings were like that. I could cry or burst out in anger at times, mostly at Derrick, but I needed a way to direct the passion I had, the intolerance I felt, towards injustice. It was at this time I got involved in a wonderful project: running a Survivor's Group. A "survivor" is a person who has been involved as a human trafficking victim, who is no longer a victim, but who has gained freedom and now must learn to support themselves (and the children they may have brought with them out of that way of life). I had help to escape the family that held me captive, and I thank God for the Task Force, but I had to learn to live on my own, to break from that victim mentality, and live the dream that was still inside of me. This passion to truly live my life burned so furiously in my heart that I knew I had to use it to help others, to set their passions on fire, to challenge them to stop depending on others and the system and do more than just survive.

Amy Returns

In 2009, my first case manager, Amy Henry, returned from Africa. She began working with The Salvation Army. I was so happy to see her again. Lucy was still my case manager, but I was doing well enough to graduate the Task Force program the following year, no longer requiring a case manager. Amy and I would get together from time to time just to visit and talk about life. That's when I told her how much I wanted to help others who had been in my situation.

Amy had been to a Survivor's Caucus, a community of survivors of human trafficking who gathered together to encourage peer-to-peer mentorship and survivor-led advocacy groups, and she really saw a need for something like this that could be implemented with the HTTF. I was thrilled she thought of me to be a part of getting that started. "I see the passion in you, Shari. You have such a strong fighting spirit in you. Really, you're a feisty, stubborn girl—just what is needed to help other survivors become more independent, like you," Amy said with a smile. I knew what she was talking about. She had known me as both the shy, scared victim I had been when I first escaped and as the stubbornly outspoken survivor that I was today.

"What if survivors could meet together to encourage one another, learn life skills, make connections?" Amy continued. "Many survivors, even though they have gone out on their own, still have many needs. Hopefully, we can fill this gap and bring them together to build relationships and help them to face everyday challenges."

Eventually, Mimi, a Task Force administrator, and Patricia, a Salvation Army administrator who volunteered with the Task Force, would be involved. "It should be survivor led, but we could have volunteer facilitators help with setting up some life skills workshops and inviting survivors willing to attend," Amy suggested. "Any outside help such as setting up a workshop on budgeting or whatever, staff can help with," Mimi chimed in. This idea was so exciting, I could hardly think of anything else. Maybe I hadn't been able to stand up for myself all of those years I was a slave, but I could be a big voice now. "I want to do this. Yes, I do this!" I told them.

The first group met at The Salvation Army Office. Patricia

and I were there. Just a few attended. But over time, more and more survivors came. I wanted the focus to be on fun things like connecting to each other and solving problems; not on being a victim, but on being a survivor.

Meetings lasted two hours or more. The format was casual. People introduced themselves. They shared their stories, if they were comfortable talking, and we had snacks and drinks. Group leaders took turns leading, so each meeting was a little different. We addressed things like cooking, finances, parenthood, or other life skills. I never missed a meeting, and I spoke to each group, letting them know that we were all here for each other. We talked about our needs. Do you need a job? Are your bills getting paid? How are your kids doing? Is your support group of friends growing?

Cooking Class

"Vickie, maybe you teach cooking for the Survivor's Group? Maybe bake something?" I asked my friend. She now had three kids of her own, and she was so patient with them. "I think that would be fun! We could have a Christmas-themed meeting," she said. "We can meet at my house." This is how most of our survivor meetings were: filled with encouragement, fun, and a friendly atmosphere.

It was mostly women who attended the groups, but we did have a man come once, for a while. Those who attended were from every nationality—English, Taiwanese, Mexican, Chinese, Romanian, Russian—human trafficking is a world-wide problem.

Survivors Groups

People who are survivors feel so lost. They get free and then realize they don't have any skills. How do they meet people, get jobs, feel connected? I am so proud of being involved in leading Survivor Groups.

My Own Child Care Business

Goals are important in our survivor's meetings, and my support system encouraged me to continue with my own. By now, I had had a couple of jobs working with preschoolers, and I really liked it. I was good at it, and I was able to take a few classes to learn more about child care. I decided I wanted to open my own child care business.

There is a lot of paperwork involved with starting your own business. In order to get my child care license, I had to read through the materials and write out my answers. I needed help. "We don't normally do this, but why don't you take the paperwork home to study? Bring it all back when you've completed it," the lady said. I was able to get a friend from church to read the materials to me and help me write my answers out. I knew how to take care of kids, and I had already done CPR and everything else; it was just the reading and writing that got in the way of me getting through the licensing process on my own. Once I did, I was allowed to care for eight toddlers or four infants. I chose infants. Administrative things like billing clients are still hard for me. I work hard to stay on top of all this.

My Name is Also Freedom

I remember some of those wonderful parents who took a chance on a new child care business like mine. My first three infants—Lilly, Big Bobby, and Little Bobby— were so sweet. They taught me so much! I remember Big Bobby cried and cried until he was able to trust me. I learned how to be patient with them and with myself. Most importantly, they taught me how to receive love.

The Interview

My life was becoming more independent. I still struggled in certain areas, but I was feeling more confident about what I wanted in my life. That is when an incredible opportunity came my way.

"CNN approached me, Shari, asking if any survivor was ready to give them an interview, and I thought of you," Mimi said to me one day in 2011. "I know you wanted to find your family. This might be the way to do it."

Community members often asked the Task Force if any survivor might want to speak, so having CNN ask to interview one of us wasn't unusual. Mimi helped as a go-between with the consulate for interviews, so we would know in advance what questions they would ask me. She did the same thing for me, too, after I agreed to do the television segment. My former case manager, Lucy, also did an interview, so she walked me step by step through the process.

CNN had a special segment called *The CNN Freedom Proj-*

ect: Ending Modern-Day Slavery, where they highlighted the issue of human trafficking. Martin Savidge was the host. He interviewed survivors of human trafficking from all over the world, and the segment would be broadcast worldwide.

Becoming Isabel

"Let's get some video of her riding her bike since she can't drive," one of the camera crew suggested. I had learned to ride a bike when one of my friends decided to teach me one day. My first bicycle was a Hello Kitty bike. My case manager thought it would help me to get around long distances. This bike was a big expense. It cost $400. I got it from a shop near the beach. I can't tell you how many times I crashed on that thing! I didn't know how to stop, at first. If I stopped, I fell. So I kept on going. It was scary. All the cars would stop for me, honk, and get mad when I would cross in the middle of the street. I would shout out to them, "I sorry! I cannot stop!" It took me only two weeks to learn. I was so short, my legs never touched the ground. I rode that bike to work nearly every day after that, even when it rained.

"We'll add a voice-over with info on her story." The CNN crew continued discussing how they would shoot the interview. I remembered the name Isabel from a girl I'd had in child care, and I liked that name, so I decided to use that name instead of mine, hoping no one would find out who I really was. That became the title of the interview: "Isabel's Misery Touches a Nation." There were shots of me riding my bike (a newer one, as the Hello Kitty bike had

215

long since been given to a neighbor's daughter); me reading a baby's storybook; the inside and outside of my apartment; and finally, me answering Martin Savidge's questions.

"This is the mom who sold you? And you want to find her?" he asked. I responded with, "Yes, yes." "And what would you say to her if you were to find her?"

The camera was on me. This was my chance to let my heart be known. I had no more anger, no more hate for anyone. "If I find her," I said, my voice raw with emotion, "If I find her, I say, 'Mom, I love you so much. I just want to find you.'" I began to cry.

The CNN interview aired in the fall of 2011. Within three days, reporters began showing up outside my apartment. Amy was visiting me at this time, helping me to deal with all of this. After she had left, within minutes, she was back. "There are two men who look like reporters wandering around the complex," she said. "I told them you weren't talking to the media at this time," she continued. Just then we heard knocking at the door and voices calling, "We just want to make sure Isabel is all right. Can we talk to her?" We peeked out of the window and saw reporters with cameras and microphones blocking the door. We didn't know what to do. "There is no way we can leave this place without them seeing us, Shari." So we didn't. We were trapped inside for four hours, figuring out what to do! This was so crazy!

Amy finally decided to call CSP, and they called the police. Several detectives showed up and helped us to leave. One of them remembered me. He was one of the detectives who had come to Judy's house after I had escaped that night.

This constant media craziness continued for the next few months.

From Case Manager to "Handler"

Amy started working with me again after this because many media outlets were trying to locate me. One day, Amy was out training officers in Lake Tahoe, and she got this call, "Amy, get down here right away, we have the president of Taiwan calling us!" Things just got crazier after that. The Taiwan foreign minister was in the area and wanted to meet me. Amy became my "handler," protecting me and becoming a go-between in all this excitement. The Police Department arranged for me and the Foreign Minister, Timothy Yang, to meet. Of course, Amy was there with me.

"I can help," Mr. Yang offered. Many other important people who wanted to help as well filled the room. I wasn't sure at this point if I was truly ready to find my family. I had said I wanted to, but I was scared. "When you're ready, we'll do whatever we can to reunite you with your family," he said assuredly. He was such a wonderful man. His help would prove so valuable to me. "Thank you so much," I said, as we shook hands, and cameras flashed from every direction.

217

Chapter 17

Finding My Family

I didn't realize that the CNN report would generate such a tremendous response in Taiwan. As far as I knew, I had been the first Taiwanese person involved in human trafficking who had ended up in the United States. Even Taiwan President Ma Ying-Jeou was offering to help. As news spread to every news outlet in Taiwan, speculation about my story grew. Could I really be telling the truth? Was I just making all this up for the money? My family back in Taiwan found it hard to avoid exposure. I had no control over how this would affect me or them or especially the truth. The Taiwan media was going wild! I would be in the news there for over a year. Some of what the media said there was not so kind.

"According to 'Isabel's' own description ... she did slave labor, was physically and verbally abused ... another source considered this impossible ... not to say 'Isabel' is trying to win sympathy ... but these

My Name is Also Freedom

doubts have surfaced ... "—Mary Chow,
Dept. of Communication Studies, PhD

It was difficult to explain how I felt to someone who has always been able to speak freely. It's difficult for someone to understand the mindset of a person who was never valued as a human being, who was treated worse than a dog, whose motives were always under question, and who was constantly told that their heart is filled with evil desires.

I had been told daily that I was never good enough, that no one wanted me, and that I was lucky to get even the little that I received. I was seven years old when I became a slave. Tell a seven-year-old child that her parents sold her to a stranger, and she cannot go home again. Tell her that although she is so very little and useless, that she must prove she was worth the money spent on her. Never let her go to school, or play with friends, or play at all! Give her no toys or new clothes or gifts of any kind. Fill her head with condemning thoughts of hopelessness and despair. Make her serve you from before the sun rises into late into the night, every day of her life.

Tell me, how would that little girl turn out? Who would she become?

Many others were sympathetic to me. Reporters interviewed people on the street. "When you watch this news, it makes you want to cry. It's very moving because it has been so many years," a young Taiwanese woman said. "They're still your blood relatives. You have to come back to meet your family members," a man commented.

News outlets dug up everything they could find, locating possible family members, even interviewing overseas Taiwanese residents who lived nearby, who eventually identified Isabel as 'Hsiao-feng.'

My Sister

"Shari, turn up the sound, look—you're on TV!" Amy and I were at my apartment sitting around talking while some Taiwanese TV station was on in the background. Suddenly, a young Taiwanese woman being interviewed held up a picture of a little girl saying, "I don't understand why our sister is not calling us." Tears filled her eyes. I looked at the TV in surprise. "Do you think this is really your sister?" Amy asked. I hadn't seen any of my sisters in so long, I wasn't sure. Was this my family? Could I trust them? "I just don't know," I answered. We had seen others, too, all over the Taiwan news, claiming I that was their daughter. Amy really believed this was my sister. "Your names are so much alike, and she even looks like you!" she exclaimed.

Minister Yang had promised that, if needed, they would use DNA testing to make sure I found my true family. I was so excited, yet so nervous inside. The love I felt for my mother and family was real, but the truth was that they had sold me as a slave. Did *they* want to see me again? What would I say, how should I act? So many questions filled my head that my stomach began to ache. I was given a contact number but hadn't got up the courage to call them yet.

My Lunlun

Through the media, the word came that this sister was mine and that my mom had been found, but she was seriously ill. She had cancer. How could this be? It took me so long to finally find her! This prompted me to make a decision: I had to go to Taiwan to see her.

I wanted to talk to my mom on the phone first. Still having some doubts, I wanted to be sure this really was her. I asked Amy to be there with me for support. I had no real furniture because of my childcare business, just toys, so we sat on the floor. I called the number Mr. Yang had given me.

The phone rang several times. There was a sixteen-hour difference in time, so it was the next morning in Taiwan. "Hello?" I said in Chinese. It was my sister who answered. There were excited squeals as we reconnected after years of being apart. We briefly talked, but I was so anxious about my mom. After a minute or two, she put her on the phone. "My Lunlun? Is that you?" I hadn't heard that name since I was so very little. My heart jumped, and I gasped out loud. I knew right then it was my mother. I struggled to speak to her, as I was beside myself with joy. It was my mom. I was here, and I was free, and I had found my mom! I had seen this day in my head over and over through the years, and I was now living it. It didn't seem real. I wanted to be there with her and hug her and tell her how much I loved her. I wanted to tell her how I had forgiven her and that now we could be a family again. "How are you?" she asked, "I missed you, too. You come soon?" She went back and forth between our native Paiwanese dialect and Mandarin, so it was hard to understand her. It wasn't a long conversation, but it was so powerful to me. I had found my mom!

"I did it, I finally did it!" I shouted when I hung up the phone. "I found my mom!"

MOFA Claims Isabel Calls Birth Mother

"Isabel, the Taiwanese woman who … worked as a domestic slave in the U.S., finally called her birth mother in Taiwan earlier this week, expressing her wish to return to the country to visit her family in eastern Taitung. Isabel … sincerely worried of her 71-year-old mother's health condition, spoke in Mandarin, repeatedly telling her mother she really misses her, while her mother emotionally asked her daughter to come back home soon."
—*China Post*, December 2, 2011

The Ministry of Foreign Affairs and Timothy Yang sped up the passport process in order for me to return quickly to Taiwan. "This should take a few days, but don't worry, we'll get it done," they told me. And they did! Not only that, but they arranged to pay for all of my flights, hotels, and whatever I needed. I was so thankful for this! Amy would come with me, as well as Derrick. My lawyer, at that time, also rearranged his schedule to make sure he could also come along. I had one more person I needed to come with me: Sister Marianna.

"Will you go back to Taiwan with me to find my family?" I had asked Sister Marianna so long ago. She knew I couldn't write in any language, so reading any of the signs or train schedules would be impossible for me. The Chinese language is the same written, but not when spoken. One word in Chinese can be pronounced in so many different ways and there are over 100 different dialects. If it is *written* down, everyone can understand it. "How can you find your mother then?" she had asked. But I would not give up. "Go with me?" She looked at me with a smile on her face. "Definitely, but will you walk from person to person and ask, 'Are you my mother? Are YOU my mother?'"

We just laughed about it, but I knew that if I went, Sister Marianna would be there with me.

January 19, 2012

I arrived in Taiwan. When we left the U.S., there had been a mob of reporters at the airport, following me around, but in Taiwan, the media waiting for me was overwhelming. The Taiwan media bombarded us the entire time—it was so crazy! My little support group went with me everywhere, just to keep me from being trampled by them!

Because the Taiwan government hosted this trip, they came up with an itinerary. Amy made sure that I understood everything. It was unheard of for a survivor to be accompanied by a case manager to go to another country. Amy was such a good friend. The Taiwan government assigned us a personal assistant and interpreter to keep us to our itinerary and to help with travel. She was Paiwanese, a shy girl, with no experience with reporters. She was kind and thoughtful and stayed with us for two weeks.

Each morning, she came to my room to tell me the schedule of where we were to go that day. I really hit it off with her the first time I talked with her. "Ms. Ho, we have a meeting today," she would say. She always made me feel comfortable. I trusted her.

Bodyguards were assigned to me. Going anywhere was so difficult. The bodyguards were even outside of my hotel room. If I went to the bathroom in a restaurant, they'd follow me and stand outside and wait. Even on New Year's Eve, they never left my side. They had guns, too. They sat in a chair in front of my hotel door, so they could make sure I was safe. They wore suits and glasses, and they were huge! "I feel so sorry, you have to stay always with me. I bring you some food," I said one night after they'd been standing, guarding me, for hours. "You don't have to wear those clothes every day, you know, for me. Wear something comfortable," I smiled. I really liked those guys.

From Slave to Celebrity

It didn't take me long to get used to all the attention. I felt like a movie star! At first, I was more serious. "Thank you," I repeated over and over in English. But soon it became kind of fun to be the center of attention. I smiled, laughed, and joked when someone asked me a question. "You are handling this really well," Amy told me one day. She spent the whole time dealing with the media, who continued to surround us so closely at times, she had to physically push people away. Amy took care of the logistics and spoke for me whenever she could. I was famous, and everyone wanted to know what I had to say. It was scary and exciting, all at the same time.

We stayed in very nice hotels, free of charge. We went everywhere, but all I could think of was seeing my family.

Reunited

We did a lot of traveling, especially since my family lived in Dawu Township, near Taitung. So many memories came back to me—some good and some bad. Where my family lived was more country and remote, so we flew into Taipei and then flew to a smaller airport. Officials met us there and drove us to where my family lived, which was quite a drive. Once a reporter asked Derrick some questions: "What do you do for a living?" He was an engineer, so they were really impressed. They asked so many questions about untrue rumors, and we ignored those.

Finding my Family

The press was always there, wherever I was, recording my reactions to everything. I was nervous about meeting my family for the first time. How would I respond? I had been separated for so long, I felt such a mix of emotions. The hardest part, which never crossed my mind would be a problem, was the cultural difference. I was raised by a woman who was Chinese, claiming to be a Christian. She had customs and did things so very differently than my family, who were native Paiwan. There were things expected of me that I had no idea I was supposed to do; ways I was supposed to act, but didn't. I had to learn how to be a sister again. I was trying to find my way back to my family and back to a culture I could not remember. Although they were my family, they were also strangers to me. Everyone had different memories about the past. We weren't sure about each other.

When I saw my family, I was so happy! Of course, we started off with hugs. I hugged my sisters and told them how much I loved them. I saw family I never knew existed and those I barely remembered. "I love you all so much. You are my family. I am now with you again." When I said this, tears and hugs began all over again.

"Where is Mom?" I asked. My mother traveled back and forth from the mountain to my sister's home. She stayed with my 3rd sister more and more often because of her health. She had remarried her first husband and both were in their seventies now.

My Name is Also Freedom

I will never forget when I saw my mother again after all of those years. "Lunlun," her frail voice said to me. This was my mother!

I put my hands on her shoulders and patted them lovingly, then rested my head on her neck. I couldn't help smiling. My mom wore a bright yellow blouse and sweater, but I could see the redness in her eyes, as if she were holding back tears. My sisters, my family, and my friends who came with me surrounded us, but so did the media. Over forty reporters watched as we stood in front of the door of my family's home, their cameras and microphones everywhere. I know the nation wanted to see this reunion, too. They had been touched by my story, but I wanted some quiet moments with my mom and family. After I felt they had enough photos, I asked, "I just want to spend time with my family ... have privacy. I know everyone is worried about me, but I just want a couple days with my family, okay?" I spoke in English. I hoped that they would understand and honor what I asked of them.

We celebrated by eating traditional food, better than what I had as a child when I lived with them. We talked, and I introduced my friends and told them about my life in America. I was able to tell my mom some of what happened to me. I could see in her face how sorry she felt that I went through all this, although she didn't say a word. Later she would tell me, "I sent you away in hope of a better life."

My Father's Grave

"You were not allowed to stay the proper time when Dad was buried," my sisters said to me. "We must go and tend to his grave. Go with us, sister."

By this time, I was very tired of the media hounding me, so my sisters and I decided to go to our father's grave site earlier than planned. "Amy, Amy," I whispered. "I go with my sisters, but I will be okay." It was just before sunrise, and Amy was still in bed. "Where are you going?" she asked, half asleep. "I go to grave with my sisters. No worry. I am okay," I assured her. I had to leave quickly, as the media was camped outside, waiting for me to go somewhere. I knew Amy would be there later, and I hoped that as she left with everyone else, the press would follow them instead of us. We sped off, found a place to park, and climbed up the hillside. I wasn't prepared for the emotions that spilled out of me. We had customs in our culture: the pouring of my father's favorite drink, the placing of items of food and such on his grave. As we each played our part in honoring our father, I suddenly began to cry. I sobbed and wept. I couldn't control myself. My sisters, each in turn, held me as I bawled and bawled. I don't think I was crying this hard for my father's loss so much as for the loss of everything else. There were so many things my family had lost because of poverty and slavery. Things could have been so different, but they were not.

The Deal

The media showed up soon after we did, and they were completely

229

obnoxious. They shouted, pushed, and shoved to get up the dusty hillside. Sister Marianna, Derrick, and Amy arrived at the same time. Sister Marianna tried to stand between my family and the reporters just as we began praying. "Could you just give them a little time? Then they will pose for you," she asked. "No," one reporter rudely responded. *Oh, want to pick a fight?* she thought, and picked up a branch off the ground and waved it so he couldn't get a clear picture of the family. When he glared at her in a threatening manner, she dropped the branch.

Amy took over from there, saying, "If this were happening in your family, would you do this?" She was also now blocking the narrow path so they couldn't pass. Finally, they replied, "No." They were upset because my sisters and I had left early and ditched them. Then Amy offered them a deal: "If you let her have this time with her family, we promise to let you know what happens; we won't mislead you again." So they left us alone.

My 3rd Sister's Wedding

When I had told my family I would be coming to Taiwan, my 3rd sister thought this would be the perfect time to have her wedding. It would be a celebration, so family from everywhere, including everyone in the village, would be there. The media drooled at an event like this.

The wedding was to begin at 9:30 a.m., but by noon there was still no progress. By 3 p.m., tables were finally set up. I felt a lot of pressure on me. I didn't know what was expected of me, culturally, and I was buying gifts, jewelry, and spending so much money. I often looked to Sister Marianna for financial advice. "Set a limit on what you are going to spend and stick to it," she'd say.

The Rooster

My mom had a rooster chained up outside who crowed every morning. We joked that this was my mother's alarm clock. Later, as the reception began, as we were all talking and laughing, I asked them, "What happened to the alarm clock this morning? He sleeping on the job?" Everyone looked at the plates of food we had in front of us. "You're eating him," they said.

We all dressed in traditional clothes for the wedding. They even gave Derrick a traditional gown and hat. We looked great! They gave me the chance to speak, as well. It was a wonderful time with my family that I will not forget.

The Letter

"What's this?" I asked, as my sister pulled a letter out of an envelope, smoothed down the edges, and held it in front of me. "I can't read it, sister. Tell me what it says." She looked at me and said, "That 'family' sent this to us." Line by line, she read the lies The Old Lady had written. It was a letter stating that Sharon was in the U.S. and was healthy, and that she "just wanted to let them all know she was okay." I was shocked. I had never known The Old Lady had been in contact with my family, that she had known where they lived and had kept this from me. "We wrote the 'grandma' back, saying that we were glad our sister was doing well, but to let her know that our mom was not in good health." I blew up and began to shout, "How she not tell me this? She knew my mom was sick and did not tell me?!" How angry I was to hear all this. The stress of this news added to all of the other feelings I was experiencing at the time. My hands shook, and it was hard to calm down. "How could she do this to me?!"

The Bike Ride

The scenery was so beautiful, we all decided to go on a bike ride, thinking it would help to calm me down a bit. Sister Marianna didn't want to go. "I can't ride a bike very well," she said. "I only know how to go straight, not turn." I knew what that was like. "Come on, go with us. We'll have fun!" I told her. "Okay," she finally said. "I'll go and kill myself!" We had to cross a big street with lots of people. We just rode right across and never looked back. Poor Sister Marianna! Derrick peeked back several times to see if she was okay. "Derrick," she later told him, "You have a good heart. You were the only one who looked back to see if I was okay."

The Woman's Shelter

"While we're here, let me contact The Salvation Army. Maybe you could share some of your story with them?" Amy said. There was a local woman's shelter that housed women who had been abused and had nowhere to go. I knew I had to speak and encourage them. "Yes, I want to do this," I said. Amy arranged the meeting, and we went. The women were from many countries, not just Taiwan. I remember looking in their eyes and understanding their pain. I loved these women, and after speaking to them, letting them know how valuable and loved they were, I knew this was what I was supposed to do in my life. "I will come back one day," I promised, as I gave each one a hug.

Falling Apart

Several times during the trip, I would have moments where the past would get hold of me. The worst one occurred when I wanted to stay closer to my family in the mountains. We needed a hotel, but the one we found was run-down and unclean. There were a few stairs, and white sheets that looked dingy and used. And there was this smell—I can't describe it. It just didn't look clean. I didn't want my clothes to touch anything. I didn't want to take my clothes off at all.

Up until now, I had tried to control most of my feelings, but as we walked into the room, suddenly I fell apart. "No, no, no ... I can't ... I can't stay here ... I have to get out ... I can't stay here ... " I screamed. I panicked. Memories from the past came flooding in. Derrick tried to help, but it just made things worse. He yelled and argued with everyone. "We have to move. We are not staying here!" No one wanted to be there, but he didn't know it. He thought I was being pressured to stay. That wasn't true. Were all the local hotels here this way? Nobody knew. I yelled, "Shut up! Shut up!" so he would just stop. Emotions were flying all over the place. It was just us four then: Sister Marianna, Amy, me, and Derrick. We got through it. We found another hotel over an hour away and stayed there about two nights.

Extended Stay

I had decided to stay an extra week. My lawyer had to return to the states, and Amy could only stay nine days of my three-week trip because she had to be back for work. Derrick left then as well. Sister Marianna had contacted a friend and had arranged for our trip to be longer. She had some connections in Taiwan and wanted to show me things, so if I ever returned and she couldn't be there with me, I'd be okay.

We stayed together and did all kinds of things. We were still mobbed, however, at every shop we tried to enter. Sister Marianna's friend was a famous cooking show host, and her brother was involved in television. We went places with him, and he entertained us. He took us to this night market. It was so much fun! I saw a jacket I liked very much. The girl at the shop recognized me and said, "If you take your picture with me, I'll give you a discount." Of course, I did!

More Bad Memories

"I have been to this market before," I said as Sister Marianna and I walked down the streets together. "The Old Lady took me here a lot. She would embarrass me so much by yelling at me. She'd yell, 'You never do anything right for me!'" I started to cry as I remembered

234

this. Then we turned another corner, and I saw a big sign that said, "Freedom." I wiped my tears and said, "Take a picture of me in front of the sign. I am free now."

Time to Leave

At the wedding, I'd said goodbye to most of my family and friends, except for Sister Marianna, who were returning to the states. Now, it was our turn to leave. I had promised my family I would come back as often as I could and call them all the time. We packed up our luggage and headed to the airport.

When we had arrived in Taiwan, we had stayed in VIP lounges to be away from the media. On our way back, we didn't have this access. The media swamped us! Sister Marianna didn't know what to do. It was just the two of us. She quickly called Amy to ask her to come to the airport when we landed. "You have got to come meet us. It is so crazy!" she begged Amy. Amy drove down to the airport, but ended up waiting and waiting in the car for us to get there. She saw many reporters who gathered outside and managed to give them an interview, distracting them from us. My lawyers had instructed me not to talk to the press, I was only to smile and nod.

Life After Finding My Family

When I returned from Taiwan, my life seemed so different. I had a family again! I couldn't wait to go back. I began Skyping my sisters and my mom all the time.

Sister Marianna had taught me how to use Skype. This had made things so much easier for me. I could see her now, and she didn't have to make the long drive down. When she showed me textbooks I needed to buy, she simply held up the book up for me to see, and I could find it on Amazon. Now this was coming in handy! I had so much catching up to do with my family. I was still receiving tutoring to learn to read and write and was more passionate than ever to tell my story and write my book.

Cindy, Beth, and Hannah

"Cindy, are you busy?" Jenna asked her friend as she saw her walking out of church one Sunday. "Lou and I would like to ask a favor of you. We're moving overseas, and there is a special friend of ours we'd like you to ... keep an eye on." Her eyes smiled as her husband, Lou, joined her. "We know this precious child of God who has been through quite a lot in her life. We met her in the church's human trafficking ministry. God has now called us to another work overseas, and we want to connect our dear little sister with some good, godly friends."

Three wonderful ladies came into my life that day: Cindy, Beth, and Hannah. After Lou and Jenna had told Cindy all about me, she found her good friends, Beth and Hannah, and they all decided to make me their special friend. They were all Taiwanese but came here to the states at different times in their lives, Cindy having lived in the U.S. the longest. They immediately welcomed me to join their home Bible study. They wanted to find out more about me and how they could help. "Well, I can see reading is still an issue; let's help out with that," Cindy said. "I'll look into it, and we'll schedule a day we can come over and do lessons with you." I attended the Bible study that Friday and shared my story with the group.

New Friends, New Lessons

"Why don't you get a phonics-based reading curriculum? I know a great one: *Sam I Am*," Diane told Cindy. "I used it with my kids." Cindy asked her coworker if she'd like to come with her to my house for that first lesson. The lessons would be weekly for a total of fifty weeks. For those first few lessons, I had a full house with Cindy, her co-worker Diane, Beth, and Hannah. We met after work about 6 p.m.

The lessons continued for about a year. At least two of the ladies were always there. They'd switch off each week, taking turns. When I had completed all fifty lessons, I was able to read the small book aloud without any mistakes.

Cindy once helped me to fill out a job application at Target. I was able to answer most of the questions on my own, but when it came to the section that asked about my education, I hadn't any. The manager was really nice when talking to me about it. "We don't just look at that. We look at other things, too." I didn't get the job, but I didn't feel sorry for myself. There were better things ahead for me.

Public Speaking

After the CNN story broke, I became well known. More and more people asked me to speak about human trafficking, especially at churches. My first time speaking was at The Salvation Army. I was so nervous! I couldn't write myself any notes then to help keep my speech on track, and when I did speak, I often wandered from story to story. I would only have so much time to speak, so this was a problem. Mimi (from the Task Force) helped me a lot with this, as did Amy and other friends.

I would usually start with, "I seven years old when my dad sold me into slavery." I'd be amazed at the reaction it had on those who listened. I knew this is what God wanted me to do. Each time I did this, I grew stronger and stronger. I would always make a point to tell them that I chose to be thankful, to be grateful for what God had done through it all, and to forgive, which was so hard to do at times when I felt so alone and abandoned, mistreated, and unloved. I didn't know how I would ever forgive my family, or The Old Lady and her daughter; but it was God who helped me to do this. He gave me those days of sitting in church where I could hear about His love, where The Old Lady could not pinch or kick or hit me. It was God who saw my needs when others donated clothes to me, and it was God who showed me kindness and brought Judy into my life to help me escape.

Meeting Sherry

I met Sherry Ward at a speaking engagement. A local church was looking for a survivor to speak at a special service highlighting human trafficking, and I accepted. I practiced with Mimi, going over everything I wanted to say. After I spoke, people came up to meet me. Sherry came up, too.

"Your story is unbelievable!" she said, as she reached out her hand to shake mine. I didn't know then that she had been praying about the types of books she felt God wanted her to take on with her newly formed publishing company, Square Tree Publishing. When she heard me speak, she felt God say, "Tell her story. Her message matters." I had wanted to write my book for many years, but it was painful to bring up those memories, and I needed someone I trusted enough to do it. Sister Marianna had tried to help, but I wasn't ready then. Sherry was patient. She was my friend for over a year before she asked me if I was interested in writing my story. "I am," I told her, "But I can't really write. I would need some help." I felt peace inside that she would be the one to help me get this done. "I think I know someone who could help with that," she said.

March 2015—My Book Begins

"Hi Shari, remember me from the coffee shop?" Melodie asked on the phone. "I'd like to arrange a time I can come by and talk. I'd like to record our conversations; I can listen to your story and then transcribe what you said. This will help me to write your book." Melodie and Sherry had been friends for many years. She now worked for Square Tree Publishing doing content editing but was willing to take on writing my book with me, and that's how it began. I would answer Melodie's questions—well, mostly I'd talk about whatever memories came to my mind while she listened. Later, she'd go home and listen to the recording and write everything down. She also began to interview many others in my life. This would continue for nearly three years.

I did a lot of crying during those times with Melodie. I still cry when I think of some of the things that happened to me. Melodie would stay for hours, recording everything. After just a few months I asked her, "My book done yet?" I had no idea how much work writing my story would be and how much time it would take.

Chapter 18

Finding Closure

I have gone back to Taiwan now several times to visit with my family. It has been such a joy to see my mom, to stay up late into the night gossiping with my sisters, eating the wonderful food my brother-in-law cooks over the barbecue. The time always goes by too fast, and I miss them all over again. They ask me the same thing when I am there, "Will you come back to live in Taiwan?" My answer is always the same, "America is my home now," and it's true. I love my home of Taiwan; I love my family and Paiwan culture, but I am an American—at least in practice. I have such different ways now of looking at life. I can't really explain it. I am independent, not bound by money or "what I am supposed to do." I am free, and I love making a way for myself here. I am blessed to have two home-lands and two cultures: Taiwan and America.

Writing this book was quite a project. I still don't have

the writing and reading skills I would like to have, but I continue going to school and learning when I can. After I became free and returned to Taiwan in 2012, I learned about my culture for the first time because it had been lost to me. So much history of the Paiwan people was withheld from me when I wasn't allowed to go to school. Melodie worked hard at bringing my story to life, but she felt that something was missing because she didn't understand my culture, my tribe, or my Asian roots. I knew a trip back to my homeland with my publishing team, Sherry and Melodie, had to happen. What I didn't know was all of the things God had planned for us—for me—on this trip.

GoFundMe

Many people might think that traveling back to Taiwan regularly and writing this book means I have a lot of money. The truth is that I daily trust God to provide for my rent and to pay my bills. I do not own my own home or have a fancy car (or a car at all!), or any extravagant possessions. I rent a modest apartment in a state that has a very high cost of living. I have my own childcare business, but one less infant and I might not be able to pay my rent that next month. My journey has been a rollercoaster, and I am not "rolling in the dough." Planning this trip with the team started with a fundraiser. I didn't have the money to even pay for my flight!

We set up a GoFundMe account. We had good results, but not quite enough for the ticket home. The Square Tree Publishing Team set up virtual meetings over the computer to discuss options. "Let's divide expenses three ways; that way, at least everything but the flight will be taken care of and Shari won't have to pay for that," Sherry Ward had said. I was grateful for that and for my team. Things were looking up, and I had hope that we'd actually be going on this trip.

Missing My Flight

"Where's Shari?" Melodie asked as Cindy, our interpreter on this trip, and Sherry Ward checked in their baggage. "Just got a text. She's still on her way. There's some kind of traffic problem," Sherry replied, glancing at her phone. Time was short, and we'd be boarding in just a few minutes. If I didn't get there soon, I wouldn't make it through TSA.

It was one of those kinds of mornings where nothing seemed to go right. We were all supposed to meet up at the airport, but traffic was unusually busy. A huge accident had brought all the cars to a stop. "Do something!" I shouted to the driver, as he wove through the lanes, trying to get around the bottleneck ahead. "I can't believe this!" I repeated over and over again, as I texted Sherry with my progress. It was going to be a close call, but I was able to get to the airport just in time to make my flight.

"Sherry," I cried, speaking into my cell phone. "I am here, but I can't get my ticket. The machine. I can't ... " Tears formed in my eyes. The trip I had wanted for so long was unraveling before me. I couldn't operate the kiosk to print out my ticket, and time was running out. I started crying. No one was helping me, for they had no idea I still struggled reading English and Mandarin. "Calm down, Shari, it's gonna be okay," Sherry repeated in her calm, confident voice. "We'll get you on the flight." But things seemed to get worse. "I am sorry. We may be able to get you on another flight, although it looks like the next one is completely full," the attendant said, clicking away at her computer. By the time Sherry Ward had made it downstairs to help me check in, the doors for boarding were shut. Melodie and Cindy were on the flight, but Sherry and I were struggling with the airline to find another flight. Thank God Sherry wouldn't take no for an answer! She found another attendant and pleaded our case. After four hours in line after line, our efforts to get on the next flight finally paid off. Two tickets were available, but they would cost an additional $600. I felt so bad for all of the trouble and extra expense I had caused, and I kept saying over and over again, "I so sorry, Sherry ... so sorry ... " but she wouldn't let me dwell on it. "All right, you have five minutes to feel bad over all of this and then we'll never talk about it again, ok?" She was determined not to let anything stop this trip and did not want me to bring these feelings with me to Taiwan. Sherry and I hung out that night in the airport, laughing and talking, and knowing that God was still at work behind the scenes to make this trip work out. We did our first Facebook live, and I began to get excited about seeing my family again. "Thank you," I said quietly, once we had finally boarded, and we were sitting in our seats. I took a deep breath and closed my eyes. It was late. This was a redeye flight, and I didn't want to miss a moment of this trip.

Mixed Emotions

Fourteen and a half hours is a long time, so I had plenty of time to think. This was not my first time coming back to Taiwan, but this was going to be the first time tracing my steps as a young girl, down the street where I lived with The Old Lady, walking through the marketplace where she'd hit me and poke me as I carried her heavy bags. It was the first time I'd see Yangmingshan again, the mountain spa The Old Lady and I journeyed to daily, and I knew that trip would bring up memories. I had to do it, but I had mixed feelings in doing it. I was quiet, not my usual talkative self. I was thinking, processing it all. My mind went back to that first trip I had taken back to Taiwan.

"Hsiao-feng, Hsiao-feng! Here! Look over *here*!" The voices had shouted from every direction, and the explosions of light from cameras everywhere had blinded my eyes. That first trip had taken place in a media frenzy! There had been fifty reporters waiting for me when I arrived at Taoyuan International Airport. I remembered the knitted wool cap and dark sunglasses I had worn, trying to hide who I was and why I was there. I wondered if anyone would recognize me when we landed this time. I closed my eyes again and heard only the roar of air and engines until I fell asleep.

Our Lodgings

I was still so tired when we went through customs and found a cab to drive us to the Airbnb. I had this really big suitcase filled with clothes and presents for my family. As I pushed it along, I must've looked pretty funny, for the bag was nearly as big as me! Cindy had booked all of our rooms for the trip and taken care of all of our travel details. I was okay with whatever she arranged. I was stunned as I opened the door to place she had rented. The layout was exactly like the place I had lived in with The Old Lady! I hardly said a word that first day. Then I finally told my team. "I remember this room," I said, as I walked slowly down the hall. "The Old Lady had a back room just like this one." I opened the door, revealing a pair of bunk beds. "There were beds like these, too, in there, and some stuff being stored, by her son I think," I continued. "It's so weird ... yeah, weird, looks the same ... " My eyes grew wide as I remembered that place. "The Old Lady ... she had those beds, but she wouldn't let me sleep in them. I had to sleep on the floor. She could've given me a room and a bed ... " Tears welled up in my eyes as the memories returned. This was such a strange feeling. It was like seeing the past, walking through a movie, but I did not feel afraid. I did not feel the same sadness like I had then. Sherry, Cindy, and Melodie were here. I am free now. I am writing my story, and this memory could not hold me hostage again. "Seriously?" Sherry asked. "Wow! No way!" I began to share many more memories, the color of the door, the flight of stairs up to the rooms. So many memories flooded in, but it was as if God Himself was here with me, with my friends, so I could face this with strength and healing.

Late Night Conversation and Joy

I found myself talking late into the night about these memories and how I felt about this trip. A healing was happening deep inside me that was new. So often in the past, the healing was painful, slow, and sometimes, explosive. This was different. Joy was forming over the wounds. I had no idea that this whole trip would be one healing

246

after another.

At times, my quietness would fade, and a bubbly joy began to take its place. "I want to cook you a traditional meal from my culture tonight," I announced the next morning. "I need to go to the street market to get what I need." The first thing I thought of was chicken feet in a warming ginger broth. "I'll go with you," Melodie blurted out quickly. We grabbed our keys and purses and headed out the door. We made our way down the stairs and out through the heavy metal door. As it slammed shut, and we walked down the sidewalk, Melodie said to me, "Okay, I'm going with you, but on one condition: I get to carry all the bags." A smile broke out over my face. I knew God was doing another healing moment in me, so I excitedly said, "Okay, Meldee, let's go!"

The street was filled with vendors and carts of all kinds. The smells were wonderful as we wove our way towards the meat vendors first. "Ohh," I said, looking at a display of various cuts of chicken. I spoke to the woman in Chinese, "I am making soup and need some chicken cut up for me." She pulled out a large half chicken and a cleaver and whacked off a meaty thigh and leg portion. She chopped it up, bones and all, and wrapped it in brown paper. I paid her, and as she gave me the package, Melodie quickly took it from me. "Oh, yeah, okay," I said, letting her carry it as we hurried on to the next vendor.

"I need vegetables," I murmured out loud. I was so excited,

it seemed as if we flew through the streets. I pointed when I couldn't remember how to say something in Chinese. The vendor placed the item in another bag, and we added it to Melodie's load. After many purchases, I knew I needed a ginger wine. I looked in shop after shop but couldn't find it. It had been so long since I had been in this same market that I had trouble remembering just where that special shop was. I stopped and asked a man, who pointed towards the end of a street where less shoppers were walking around. The streets were so full of people I had to weave through, careful not to lose Melodie in the process. This was the most expensive item that I needed, so I got just a small bottle and paid for it. It felt wonderful to pay for all of these things! I may have been a slave and bore the burden the last time I had walked these streets, but not now. I was preparing a feast, and I would be both the rich lady buying it and the gracious host eating it. How wonderful this adventure was! "Wow, these bags are heavy," I heard Melodie comment. She now had about six or more plastic grocery bags, equally strung, three on each arm. "And you were how old when you carried all of these? How were you able to do it?!" she said in disbelief. "And that Old Lady just hung on your shoulder the whole time, too!" I heard every word, but my excitement carried me above them, as I still needed a few more items to make my meal complete. We passed shellfish, noodles, pork vendors, enormous flats of mushrooms, vegetables, ginger, and spices, and finally, a man making tofu, carefully scooping great bowls of the hot chunky white mixture out of huge steaming pots and pouring it into thin cloths, pressing and draining it.

Finding Closure

"Okay, I am done," I finally said to Melodie, handing her the last bag. "Let's go back so I can cook it all up!"

I couldn't stop smiling. As we passed a vendor who was selling some chicken feet, tenderly cooked on skewers, I had to buy one. "I was never allowed to have this on those trips to the market with The Old Lady. You want some?" I asked. Melodie's face squished into a "yuck, no thanks" type of face, and she shook her head. I laughed, collected my treat from the man, and munched happily on my tasty snack as we headed back to the Airbnb. I felt a strength I hadn't felt before as we walked on, and it felt good.

I love to cook when it's for the people I love and to celebrate life. The Airbnb had everything I needed to prepare this feast for my friends. I pulled out all of my wonderful treasures I had bought on the street and began cutting, chopping, peeling, and preparing the dinner. I had so much fun! It wasn't long before the place filled with the smells of my culture, and we all sat around and said a prayer of thanks. "God, I thank you for my friends, for this food, and for all you have done for me. I love my family and am so happy to be here to see them again. And God, I want to see my mom before I leave. Please, God, help me to see my mom again. Thank you, God, so much. Thank you."

Elim Publishing

"I really believe your story needs to be in Chinese, and that the people of Taiwan need to read it," Sherry Ward had told me one day.

My Name is Also Freedom

"When we are in Taiwan, I want to find a publisher, at least make a connection. Let's see what happens." My mind was on so many other things, but I was amazed when Cindy made an announcement to us at dinner. "You know I have been calling every publisher in the phone book since we got here," she said, as she sat down at the table and scooped a ladle full of the hot soup into a bowl. "Well, Elim Publishing said we could come down to their offices. They can't guarantee a meeting, but it is possible one of their staff could come out and at least meet us. They have a big bookstore with offices in town. We could go tomorrow." We had only been in Taiwan two days, and we had such an opportunity already.

The bookstore was quite a ways in town, so we decided taking the bus would be a cheaper option. The city had changed so much since I was last in Taipei. The Taiwanese love books and we first stopped at a very large bookstore that was the local hangout. It was amazing how many people were coming and going and finding places in the store to read and relax. It was so quiet in there. We all walked around and got a feel for the types of books that were popular there. "I wonder if Elim is just as big as this?" Cindy asked as we left and walked toward the street.

"Hey, here's the sign," Melodie said. Next to the large sign that said Elim was another one that said "Jesus loves you" in Mandarin. This is a good sign, I thought to myself. We went down a steep set of stairs that opened up into a very large bookstore. Displays of books, pictures, chopsticks, cups, textbooks, songbooks, even souvenirs were everywhere. I wandered around as Sherry went to find someone to talk to. It wasn't long before she returned and said, "You're not going to believe this, but the president of Elim has decided to meet with us personally." We all felt a little nervous as an assistant led us to Elder Huang's office. Books and manuscripts were piled everywhere. We sure needed Cindy, as she had to do a lot of translation for the team.

Elder Huang began asking us all kinds of questions. He was formal, but kind, yet I wasn't sure if he was interested in what my story was about. After some time, I asked if I could speak freely. I began to tell my story. "I was a very young tribal child when my parents sold me," I started. "I am from the Paiwan tribe. We lived on the mountains of Taitung. We were so very poor. My family sold me to an Old Lady, and I was abused very badly." I saw something in his eyes I had not seen before. It was almost as if he had known my story. I went on to tell more details, and when I finished speaking, he began to speak. "When I was a young college student I visited those mountains." He paused, swallowed hard, and continued. "I heard loud shouts and went to see what was happening. I saw a young girl kicking and screaming as two drunken men exchanged money and bottles of liquor and the young girl, still kicking and crying, was taken away. I couldn't believe this and asked, 'What has happened here?' I was told she was a tribal girl who was sold for money and goods. I wanted to stop this, but what could I do? I had no money to buy her or to physically fight these two men." Grief fell over Elder Huang's face. I could see his eyes watering, but he finished his story. "I have never forgotten that moment. I have tried to find that girl to this day but could not. I have always wanted to tell her story." He could no longer keep his tears from falling. As he wept, we all began to weep as well. "What is more," he went on to say, "four years ago I was diagnosed with terminal cancer. I was looking for the girl up near the villages on the mountain and some of the tribal members who were Christians asked to pray for me. I am alive and here today because of that." The whole atmosphere in the room completely changed. In moments, Elder Huang declared, "Elim will do whatever we can to publish your book here in Taiwan. When you are finished writing it, let me know." What we all felt at that moment could not be put into words.

The staff then took us on a tour of the store, and we were invited to a special traditional Taiwanese lunch and tea. I was treated like a princess that day. What could be in store for tomorrow?

The Street

"Since we are in Taipei, we should go to that street," Melodie suggested. The sky had grown cloudy as the evening came, but we had our umbrellas, so we decided to go. I was especially anxious about going there. That street was the street I lived on with the Old Lady when I had first been sold to her. It was more of a long alley rather than a street, with bar after bar down one side. I knew I had to go. "Is this it?" Melodie asked, as the bus dropped us off on the corner. It was raining steadily now, but not too hard. It made the alley look dark and dirty, just as I remembered it. Melodie and I walked together, Cindy and Sherry Ward in front of us.

"This is it," I said, as I stopped in front of a tall apartment building. It was grey and dull and looked no different from all of the rest of the buildings that dotted the street. All of us were so very quiet at that moment. I think we were all thinking about what took place in there. I looked at the window I had looked out so long ago, wondering when my mother would come and take me home. "She is never coming for you. She sold you, and you will never see her again," The Old Lady had said. My heart had been crushed. I took one last look and silently walked on. The Old Lady was dead. That life was dead. I am not a slave anymore. I will never be a slave again. I am free.

I am free.

We walked on silently for some time until we reached a small restaurant at the end of the street. We sat and ate and it was good. I was okay. I had faced that dark place and walked on into the light.

Facing Yangmingshan

There was one more place near Taipei that held extreme sadness for me. That was the natural hot springs spa that The Old Lady and I had traveled to almost daily. It had been here that I stood serving her, not allowed to move, not even to use the restroom without threats of being beaten if the Old Lady had to stop her visiting to walk me to the bathrooms. It was here that she ate all the wonderful foods from the vendors, but I was not allowed to eat any of it. It was here I threw my blood-soaked tissues down the hillside because I was not given any sanitary napkins to use. "We must take the bus up to Yangmingshan. It is steep, but then we must walk to reach the hot springs," I explained to the team. As we rode the bus, I remembered the time I found that sack lunch someone had left on the bus. I had forgotten that always-hungry feeling I used to have. Thank God I don't feel that nagging pain anymore, I thought. "Okay, this is the last stop. We walk now," I told the ladies, as we all got off the bus and walked up the steep hillside. As we walked on, we came upon the park area and the mineral pools. "We won't be able to see where the Old Lady took me inside the building where her private spa was, but that is the building over there." The park was actually quite beautiful. The large picnic tables and chairs were made of polished rocks and boulders. Small mineral streams and pools wove here and there throughout the park. Suddenly, I recognized a large tree that was cut into an unusual shape. "Mr. Tree," I said, as reached out to give this rather large and boxed-shaped tree a hug. "Do you remember me?" I asked. "I am no longer a slave, like when I first met you. I am free!" I gave the tree the biggest hug. It was as if all of the negative thoughts about this place were washed away in the waters that flowed through this park, and I was filled with new feelings of joy. I truly was free, and only this tree that once was as little as I was knew my story and had seen me back then. I had to share my joy with it.

My One Desire

Before we had left on this trip, I had told the team what was going on with my family and how I wanted to see my mom while we were in Taiwan. "I want to see my mother. I asked God to make it happen," I told the ladies. We had all been praying for this, especially Melodie, who had talked with my mom on Skype over a year ago. It may be hard for readers to understand my culture and how birth order and family structure plays such a huge role in how we interact with one another. I am the 2nd sister, but because I had been gone so long away from the family, my 3rd sister had taken on the role to care for my mom and to be there, especially when my mother was diagnosed with cancer. My relationship with my sister had been strained because of this, so I was to stay with my 4th sister during this trip. I love my family—I love my sisters. I never want anything to come between us. I pray for us all to forgive and find a way to stay as a family should, no matter what we have all gone through.

The Mountain

Where my family lives now is very different than where I spent my first seven years of life. Our home then was near the top of the mountain overlooking the beautiful Pacific Ocean. The wind had swept through the tin sheets and wooden planks that made up our 'house.' The floor was dirt and the bugs plentiful, but at least it kept us out of the elements and warm at night. I needed to go there now, to see where I was born, to remember. We had all taken the train from Taipei down to Dawu Township in Taitung. The train ride across the countryside was long, and we had to change trains, so we arrived long after dark. My 4th sister was going to meet us at the station. "Can we go out to the mountain where I was born tomorrow?" I asked her in Chinese as we drove towards the hotel where we were booked to stay. "You want to go there?" she asked back. "Yeah, okay, we can. I think I remember where. There are many changes and that house may not be there anymore." I had forgotten how windy it was away from my sister's village and up near the new highway where the old houses were. "We must stop at the beach and see that," my sister insisted. We stopped and looked around and got our bearings. After a few attempts, we finally found where the house would have been. Other houses, so much like the one I was born in, stood nearby. "We'll have to walk up the hillside. The trail is too narrow for a car," I told the team. Memories flooded back as I saw the houses. I could see myself running down the path when my father had brought home that TV. I saw the laundry blowing in the wind as my mother clipped it to the rope clothesline. I remembered my mother teaching me to make rice. As I remembered, I told my team the memories so they could see them, too. "We must go now," my sister said. "We want to see mom, if we can today." I shook off the memories and climbed down the mountainside.

The Visit

"I will take you to see her, but be prepared, you maybe not get the chance," my 4th sister told me as we got in the car." Because of family tensions, my visit with my mother was up in the air, but I knew God would work it all out. We drove across the wide highway and down through the village. The streets were narrow here, like an alley, so we drove very slowly, hoping for an opportunity to visit. This is when I saw my mother, sitting outside around back in a chair, enjoying the weather. "Mama!" I shouted. I jumped out of the car and ran to see her, threw my arms around her, and hugged her tight. "Thank you, God. I finally see my mom. I got all the wishes I wanted. Thank you so much, Jesus! Please, I ask that she would prosper and that You would take care of her." I was so excited. Before I knew it, most of my team was there with me, meeting my mother, who nodded and smiled because she only spoke her native tribal language, which even I could not completely understand.

Our visit was so short, but at least I was able to see my mother. That was what I had prayed and hoped for, and I couldn't be happier.

Family Time

Things were not yet perfect with my family, but they were changing for the better. We then headed back with my 4th sister to her house and prepared for dinner. It was a feast and filled with the culture of my people. "What is in this pot?" Melodie asked, as she gave the soup a stir.

"Tang yuan," I replied. "It is a warming soup with rice balls. I love this soup! We will start with the soup, and how many rice balls you get will tell if you are lucky or not," I explained with a grin. "My brother-in-law will also grill fish and many different meats. I know you will love it all," I said. I wanted to talk and tell her so much about my culture and family that I couldn't wait for dinner to start. "See," I explained as the fish was placed on the grill. "Outside it is covered in salt, so much it forms a crust. It steams inside this crust. The fish, so juicy!" Skewers of meats, vegetables, and wonderfully flavorful sauces were cooked and passed around. In moments, the house and yard filled with people: nieces, nephews, and neighbors from all over. I saw Melodie looking at everything. I knew she was studying it all to help make my book feel like every word was written by me. "You see this nut?" I asked Melodie, as I saw her looking at the men who were chewing and spitting something, their lips red with a juice that the nut produced.

"This is the betel nut; it is said that it gives energy to those who chew it. My tribe has chewed these for years. My mother chewed these for many years to have energy to work. This is why she has cancer now. It is from chewing the betel nut." Melodie picked one up and turned it over in her hand. "It looks like some kind of acorn to me," she said. "I guess, maybe, it is like tobacco or something. Interesting." The night continued like this, eating, talking, observing, then talking and eating some more. It was very late when the team decided it was time to head to the hotel. As Cindy, Melodie, and Sherry Ward stood up from the table, they thanked my family.

"I know we said we would all stay together on this trip," I told them, "but I want to stay with my sister tonight; I need to be with her this night." I knew they understood, although they were hesitant at first. They finally agreed, and my brother-in-law drove them back to the hotel.

I talked and shared my heart with my sister late into the night. We talked about anger and forgiveness. We talked about family and betrayal and healing and the events of the day. My sister told me, "When you came back to the family, it changed everything. God did something in our family. Sister, after you talked to me about all of this, I think I can forgive. Does everything that happens have a reason?" she asked. I thought for a minute and then said, "It was not my choice to go to America, but now I live there. I know God loves us and is working things out for us, always." We were both quiet for a moment. I know that what she had been through in her own life was terrible, for she had been sold, too. I looked at her with so much love in my heart for her and said, "We all have a different story, but our pain is the same. I want to write this book to help others. To help our family. It was hard for me, too, to forgive our parents—God helped me to do this. We must inspire others. We must help others by sharing our story."

"Do you remember what Mama used to say?" I asked. It was so late now, and we had both climbed into her big bed and pulled the blanket up close to our chins. I thought back to when I was little and had shared a pillow with her so very long ago, the same pillow I had left behind when I was sold, so she would not be without one. I felt the warmth of love towards her like I did when we were so very small. I had been her big sister, her protector, even though I was probably only six years old at the time. "Remember?" I continued, thinking of that last meal I had had with my family, the sweet chicken and the bitter herbs. "Tell me," she asked sleepily, "what did Mama say?" I curled up closer to her, resting my head on her shoulder. I rubbed my nose with the tip of the blanket and sighed satisfyingly. "Life is like this meal, Little Lunlun; it is both sweet and good, but bitter and hard. Your life will be like this, too. Always be patient. Endure and overcome, because tomorrow will always be better. Beneath the bitter herb is tender meat, to make you strong. Do not stop at the first bite; keep eating. Tomorrow *will* be better."

As I drifted off to sleep, I thought about those words. I thought about what God had done that day. I remembered something He said in the Bible, "In this world you will have trouble. But take heart! I have overcome the world." (John 16:33b)

God has done so much for me in spite of all the bitter herbs that I have tasted. Beneath my current struggles, there is sweet meat, and I will not stop until my family knows God's love, for I know tomorrow will be better!

Go to freedomhasaname.com/shari to see a video of Shari in Taiwan.

Timeline of Important Events

1542: Portuguese sailors pass Taiwan. In the ship's written log, they describe Taiwan as Ilha Formosa, which means "Beautiful Island."

1590: Chinese start settling in southwestern Taiwan (Formosa).

1603: Taiwanese natives (aboriginal tribes) are first described.

1604—1668: The Dutch, Chinese, and Spanish all lay claim to parts of Taiwan (Formosa).

1874: The Japanese invade Formosa, leading to its ultimate domination in 1895.

1905: Formosa was considered the second-most developed region of East Asia; Census records show a population of 82,795 "mountain people" living in Taiwan.

1912: Formosa officially becomes Taiwan.

1925: Taiwan is the major food supplier for Japan's industrial economy.

1937: The Chinese language is banned in newspapers and removed from school curriculums. The policy of Kōminka, "transformation," begins in Taiwan.

1944: American forces bomb Taiwan in an effort to defeat Japan during World War II.

1945: Japanese rule in Taiwan ends, and China lays claim to the island.

1949: Chiang Kai-sheik arrives from communist China, dispossessing thousands of natives. He hopes to transform Taiwan into an industrial power base to reclaim China from the communists.

1949: The Taiwan Provincial Government announces the imposition of martial law. Under martial law, Mandarin Chinese became Taiwan's official language. Anyone caught speaking in an indigenous tongue or the local Taiwanese dialect was punished. Aborigines are forced to adopt Chinese names.

1964: The Taiwanese language is banned in schools and official settings.

1980: Hsiao Feng (Shari Ho) is born.

1987: Shari's family sells her to a rich older woman as a slave. Martial law in Taiwan is lifted.

July, 1994: News of Shari Ho's father's death reaches her through a phone call.

1996: The Council of Aboriginal Affairs is established, officially recognizing sixteen indigenous tribes living throughout Taiwan, supporting culture, language, and granting recognized status to indigenous tribes.

2000: Taiwan's Immigration Act is enacted, and the Victims of

Trafficking and Violence Protection Act (TVPA) is passed into federal US law.

2002: The Council of Aboriginal Affairs changes its name to the Council of Indigenous People. There is an estimated native population of 540,000.

2004: A virtual organization known as the Human Trafficking Task Force (HTTF) is created.

August 18, 2005: Hsiao-feng (Shari Ho) escapes her captors, who file a missing person's report with the police.

August 19, 2005: Shari's photo is seen on TV. Officers show up at Judy's house.

2006: The Old Lady dies in a convalescent home.

August 18, 2006: Shari celebrates her first birthday.

2009—2010: Shari starts her own childcare business.

2010: Shari graduates from the Task Force program for Survivors and begins leading Survivor groups.

June 27, 2007: Shari faces her captors in a legal deposition. Later that night, Shari is hospitalized for a suicide attempt.

November 2011: The CNN Freedom Project interviews Shari and the program airs world-wide.

January 19 2012: Shari returns to Taiwan to reunite with her family.

March 2015: Shari collaborates with Square Tree Publishing to write her story.

January 2018: Shari and the Square Tree Publishing Team travel to Taiwan.

January 2019: Shari Ho's story, My Name Is Also Freedom, is published.

Glossary

abducted: The illegal carrying away of a person, such as the taking of a child from its parent.

aboriginal: Natives or the earliest inhabitants of a land.

abuse: To treat or speak to one in a harmful, or injurious way.

agent: A person authorized to act on another's behalf.

affidavit: A written statement, confirmed by oath and used in court.

bad luck numbers: The number 4 is bad luck in Chinese culture. The word for number 4 sounds like the word for "death" in Chinese.

baptize: To admit someone to a specific church by a ceremony where the person is sprinkled or plunged into water.

betel nut: The seed of the areca palm tree which is chewed for its nicotine properties.

Bible: A collection of sacred texts, considered a product of divine inspiration and a record of the relationship between God and humans by Christians and Jews.

birth order: The order in which a child is born into a family.

This is of central cultural value to many Asian cultures.

botanical gardens: A well-kept park than contains many different kinds of plants.

broker: A person who buys, sells, or arranges a deal.

canvassing: Questioning persons, perhaps door to door.

captor: A person who has captured another person.

capture: To take by force.

case: An investigation or file regarding a situation.

Catholic: A word meaning "universal" and a denomination of Christian religion.

Chinese: A person from China; a form of language.

Christian: A believer in Christianity; a follower of Christ.

CNN: (Cable News Network) a news reporting agency.

CNN Freedom Project: A year-long humanitarian news media campaign launched by CNN and CNN International in 2011 to "end modern-day slavery" and related illegal practices, including human trafficking.

colony: A group of people who leave their native country to form a settlement in a new land which is subject to, or connected with, the parent nation.

colonization: The forming of a colony or settlement.

communal: Shared by all members of a community.

Glossary

communion: The service of Christian worship at which bread and wine are shared.

contract: An agreement between two or more parties, enforceable by law.

CPS: Child Protective Services is the name of a governmental agency in many states of the United States responsible for providing child protection, which includes responding to reports of child abuse or neglect.

crime: Serious wrongdoing that breaks the law.

Dawu Township: A rural township in Taitung County, Taiwan, with the majority of its inhabitants being the indigenous Paiwan people.

deposition: The process of giving sworn evidence.

escape: To get away.

eavesdropping: Secretly listening to a conversation.

eccentric: Unconventional behavior.

evidence: Proof.

exploit: To selfishly use someone.

exploitation: Using a person to gain profit for oneself.

Formosa: Taiwan.

forced labor: Required to work without one's permission, usually without payment.

Governor Shimpei Goto: (1857—1929) A Japanese politician and cabinet minister who served as the head of civilian affairs of Taiwan under Japanese rule.

green card: A permanent resident card issued by U.S. immigration services.

Homeland Security: A Department of the United States government whose work includes customs, human trafficking investigations, immigration, border enforcement, emergency response to disasters, and cybersecurity.

Hsiao-feng: A mythical royal bird in Chinese that is benevolent and is said to appear only in places that are blessed with the utmost peace, prosperity, and happiness. It hides away in times of trouble. Shari Ho's given name.

Human Trafficking Task Force (HTTF): A collaboration of law enforcement, victim service providers, non-profit organizations, faith-based organizations, government entities, and the community. Its mission is to work together, taking a victim-centered approach with the common goal of combating human trafficking and related crimes.

indigenous: Native, originating from a place.

indoctrinate: To teach one to uncritically accept a set of beliefs.

illegal: Forbidden by law.

injustice: An unfair act or a violation of one's rights.

innocent: Not guilty.

interrogate: To ask questions, sometimes aggressively.

Glossary

Jesus: The central figure in Christianity, believed to be the Son of God and the awaited Messiah or Savior.

Kōminka: A policy which aimed to turn the Taiwanese into loyal subjects of the Japanese emperor.

legal: Permitted by law.

Long Shan Temple: A Chinese folk religious temple.

Lunlun: The name Shari's mother called her when she was very young.

Ma Ying-Jeou: Mayor of Taipei from 1998—2006 and President of the Republic of China (ROC) from 2008—2016.

MOFA: Ministry of Foreign Affairs.

mountain lily: Also called Formosa Lily, a plant with long, white fragrant trumpet-shaped flowers on tall, sturdy stems which blooms in mid to late summer.

Nationalists: A political group advocating for their nation and its independence.

NTD: New Taiwanese Dollar, the currency of Taiwan.

Paiwan: One of the indigenous tribes of people who are native to Taiwan.

period: Another term for menstruation, the female biological process during which the lining of the uterus discharges blood and other materials every month from puberty until menopause, except during pregnancy.

persecution: The harassing of others due to their beliefs, race, or any other differences.

poverty: Having very little or no money, goods, or means of support; poor.

primitive: An extremely basic level of comfort.

PTSD (Post Traumatic Stress Disorder): A condition that develops in some people who have experienced a shocking, scary, or dangerous event or events.

Salvation Army: An evangelical Christian church whose mission is to preach the Gospel while helping others in need without discrimination.

sexual exploitation: Abuse of another person's sexuality for the purpose of sexual gratification, financial gain, or any other non-legitimate purpose.

slave: A person who is the owned property of another.

slavery: The condition of being a slave.

smallpox: A highly contagious and deadly disease marked by a high fever and small pustules that break and leave scars.

stinky tofu: A Chinese form of fermented tofu that has a strong order.

suicide: The act of taking one's own life voluntarily and intentionally. A suicide attempt is when someone intends to end their life, but they do not die as a result of their actions.

survivor: A person who continues to function or prosper in spite

Glossary

of opposition, hardship, or setbacks; a victim of human trafficking.

Survivor's Caucus: A meeting of human trafficking survivors and support staff seeking to educate members and others on ways to combat human trafficking.

Taipei: The chief or capitol city in Taiwan.

Taitung: A city on the southeast coast of Taiwan.

Taiwan: Officially the Republic of China, ROC is a state in East Asia.

Tang yuan: A Chinese soup made with rice wine vinegar and sweet glutinous rice balls.

Tier 1: The top rating a country obtains if it complies with the Victims of Trafficking and Violence Protection Act of 2000.

tropical: Hot and humid; a region near the equator.

transcribe: Putting (thoughts, speech, or data) into written form.

trauma: An experience that produces physical or psychological injury or pain.

tribe: A group of people united by a common ancestor; aboriginal people.

TSA: The Transportation Security Administration of the United States.

turquoise: A bluish green color.

typhoon: A tropical cyclone or hurricane of the western Pacific area and China seas.

typhoon season: Rainy season from June through October.

victim: A person who suffers from an injury or is deceived or cheated by another.

Victim Witness Program: A part of Child Protective Services, offering support to victims/witnesses of crimes.

village: A small, usually rural settlement that is smaller than a town.

warrant: A document authorizing something (typically an arrest or a search).

whore: A prostitute; a person who engages in sexual activity for payment.

work visa: Permission to take a job in a foreign country.

World War I: A global war originating in Europe that lasted from July 28, 1914 to November 11, 1918.

World War II: A global war including United States, Europe, and Asia that lasted from 1939 to 1945.

Yangmingshan: A national park and hot springs located in northern Taipei City.

About Shari Ho and Melodie Fox

Shari Ho is a speaker and human trafficking awareness advocate, which led her to create human trafficking survivor groups throughout Orange County, CA. Her fight to be a voice for survivors everywhere has given her a world-wide platform, through the BBC podcast, CNN International, Orange County Register, and reaching all Asia through Asia One News International.

Melodie Fox is a writer, editor, and educator working with a non-profit educational foundation to expand STEM in her local community. Her work with Shari Ho has led her to speak and travel on behalf of human trafficking survivors, and promote awareness of this global crisis on such international platforms as CNN International.

For more information or to have them speak at your event, contact
Square Tree Publishing at
info@squaretreepublishing.com

Made in the USA
Middletown, DE
28 March 2021